D0317765

DAVID WATSON –
A PORTRAIT BY HIS FRIENDS

Also by Edward England
  An Unfading Vision
  The Spirit of Renewal
Other Highland Books
By Paul Tournier
  The Adventure of Living
  Escape from Loneliness
  A Doctor's Casebook in the Light of the Bible
  Secrets
  Marriage Difficulties
  A Place for You
  The Strong and the Weak
By Michael Green
  Evangelism in the Early Church
By Edith Schaeffer
  What is a Family?
By John L. Sherrill
  They Speak with other Tongues
By Phyllis Thompson
  A London Sparrow
By Thomas à Kempis
  The Imitation of Christ (A Modern Reading)
By Oswald Sanders
  Prayer Power Unlimited
By Michael Harper
  Walk in the Spirit
By F. F. Bruce
  Paul and his Converts
Edited by Edward England
  A Way with Words

DAVID WATSON

A PORTRAIT BY HIS FRIENDS

Edited by

EDWARD ENGLAND

HIGHLAND BOOKS

Printed in Great Britain for
HIGHLAND BOOKS
Crowton House, The Broadway, Crowborough,
East Sussex TN6 1AB,
by Cox & Wyman, Reading
Typeset by Nuprint Services Ltd, Harpenden, Herts.

CONTENTS

It is the wish of the editor and contributors to this book that all royalties should go to David Watson's family.

FOREWORD

by

Lord Coggan

An autobiography sheds light on the writer from within. A biography focuses the light from without. David Watson has provided us with autobiography in his books *You Are My God* and *Fear No Evil*. This set of essays is, in some respects, like a biography, in that each essay focuses a ray of light from an outside source on a man whom God greatly used. Together these rays of light give a very fair impression of David's character and work.

There is triumph in this book. There is sadness. There is humour. There are lessons to be learnt, particularly from such a shrewd and constructively critical assessment as that by John Poulton.

Any thoughtful reader will finish the book a more thankful and a more humble person than when he began it. And this is what David would have wanted and what Anne, who has graciously allowed the book to be put together, undoubtedly desires.

INTRODUCTION

'The Christian gospel is not about superstars,' David Watson wrote, 'but about God's extraordinary grace in spite of very human faults and failure.' In this volume twelve of his friends have portrayed the man as they knew him, being unsparingly frank as he would have wished. They tell of his outstanding qualities as pastor, evangelist and communicator, demonstrating in his own words 'that no human frailty need hinder God's infinite grace.'

David Watson wrote two autobiographical books *You Are My God* and *Fear No Evil*. In the first he told the story of his first fifty years; in the second of the last fourteen months. Dr J. I. Packer described *You Are My God* as 'a painfully honest record, full of God, in the manner of 2 Corinthians.' We hope this book is both as honest and as full of God. It is a thanksgiving and a celebration. A thanksgiving to God for giving David to us; a celebration that 'those who belong to God shall live again.'

Several publishers wished to commission a biography after David's death. At the request of his wife, Anne, it was decided that such an indepth book, if it were to be written, should be delayed for four or five years until an objective assessment could be made. This volume, in the

11

meantime, portrays the man who pioneered a worship, renewal and evangelistic mission that reached out from York to affect Christians around the world.

I would like to thank Lord Coggan for his foreword, Lord Blanch for permission to reproduce the address he gave at the Thanksgiving Service in York Minster, and Anne Watson for her encouragement and support. Carolyn Richardson, Highland Books' editor, has prepared the typescript for the printer.

Edward England

Chapter One

A PERSONAL VIEW

by

David MacInnes

Canon David MacInnes has been involved in evangelism in university missions and renewal since the 1960s. He is canon missioner for the Anglican diocese of Birmingham.

'I would love you to meet someone who has recently become a Christian. I think he would find your friendship an encouragement'. It was David Sheppard speaking, and like many another Cambridge undergraduate at the time, I was secretly pleased to be noticed and *wanted* by the unusually handsome cricket captain of both Sussex and England. We fixed a time to meet in his rooms, and a couple of days later I was introduced to the 'someone'.

David Watson, as it turned out to be, seemed very typical of a circle into which I had been introduced the previous year. We had a fair amount in common. From a similar sort of pedigree and public school background, I too had been commissioned into the Royal Horse Artillery for my national service, and so we began by self-consciously exchanging the conversational visiting cards ('Oh! you led your guns into a bog in Germany did you? So did I!') which are designed to protect oneself, whilst cautiously seeing if a point of real contact can be found. It's rather like two dogs sniffing each other, each uncertain about the other's temperament and fangs though quite pleased with the evidence of familiar canine smells and habits! It soon became clear to me, in that short introductory half-hour, that David 'smelt' Christian! St.

Paul talks about disciples carrying the fragrance of Jesus, the aroma of Christ, and it was that scent which was to grow stronger and stronger around David eventually until it poured out from him.

But if smell is one thing, friendship is quite another! Whilst I liked the former, I was not too sure how far I could go with the latter. I dutifully carried out the fellowship role that David Sheppard had sketched, periodically inviting David round for coffee or going to a Bible reading with him. Beyond that, however, we did not naturally get drawn together. I think he probably found me far too scatty. I found him far too correct. He loved wearing his old Wellingtonian tie! Whilst I struggled to keep a daily time of prayer, he could flaunt a long prayer list, and was devouring an intolerably well balanced diet of devotional, doctrinal and biographical Christian books as well. Perhaps because I find it hard to discipline myself, it was threatening to find a contemporary who was so quickly conforming to the accepted pattern of evangelical piety. My contempt for conformity was partly due to my personal failure to reach the expected standards. But David did conform. Whether it was regular attendance at Bible readings every Saturday evening at the Cambridge Union or renouncing the taboos of the day, he did it! ('Never serve any other king but Jesus—not Drin-King or Smo-King' was the characteristic advice given by the Rev E. J. H. Nash, one of our inimitable mentors). My worm's-eye view at the time was that this was the pathway to arid and empty Christian Union convention. But in fact, God was at work in David's life forming a deep channel of discipline through which his grace was to flow out most powerfully in the following years. What was immature dogmatism and restricting legalism in those early days, was later to be transformed by his experience of the Holy Spirit and his careful study of the Scriptures. Meanwhile that radiating love for Christ, which held many spell-bound at celebrations all over the country in the late seventies and early eighties, had been tested against the practical alternatives of youth such as films, girlfriends and parties. He had reached the firm conclusion that Christ is the pearl of great price, and that he is worth any sacrifice.

I discovered another foundation-stone of David's Christian life at that time. David and I were sitting amongst the spring crocuses on the banks of the river Cam—the sort of idyllic setting where students either get swept away with romantic fantasies, or start flapping their little academic wings and talking philosophical nonsense. As there were no pretty girls in distress floating helplessly down the river, I found myself expounding some form of intellectual clap-trap. David, who had a clear mind, listened patiently until I had finished. He didn't attempt to demolish my arguments or even dismiss them. Instead, he talked about his own thinking. He described to me the kind of struggle he had been through during his teens, weighing up the teaching of Christian Science, which had led to the death of his father when he was only ten, and then the attractions of theosophy, Buddhism and various forms of eastern mysticism. These had all spoken of a spiritual reality beyond man, but over against them stood human reason and the scientific method which had exercised a magnetic pull upon him too. Were they really the only valid way of discovering truth? If so, they left more doubts than certainty when it came to the great question of God. Was faith then to be left in the hands of the emotions rather than the mind? 'I have come to the conclusion' he said, 'that in the end, we have got to trust God's revelation of himself. Human thinking is always relative. The only way to find out if a thing is true or false, is to test it against the person of

Jesus Christ who we find in the Scriptures.' So he devoted his mind to the study of the Bible and that became the bedrock of his ministry. Many years later, a man who was going through a period of turmoil found himself listening to David at St Michael-le-Belfrey in York. 'What impressed me most' he related afterwards, 'was David's burning enthusiasm which came from such a scholarly study of the text of Scripture. It was so exciting to see how clearly that passage of the Bible applied to me.' It was Dr Martyn Lloyd-Jones who described preaching as 'theology coming from a man who is on fire.' From the early days of his Christian life, David began to allow his mind to be shaped and fired by the Scriptures.

I had served a year as a curate in Gillingham when in 1958 Bishop Chavasse of Rochester, who had seen in the Rev John Collins an excellent trainer of young clergy, suggested that St Mark's should have a second assistant. For a church which five years before had been badly run down, and had no curate at all, this was exciting evidence of new life and growth. The treasurer of the PCC, however did not see the matter in that light at all. This, as far as he was concerned, was going to be an intolerable burden on the finances. So, although David Watson, who had just completed his theological course at Ridley Hall, had been recommended as 'a very able person indeed', he decided on outright opposition to the appointment as a matter of principle. Several of the older lay people had already found the new emphasis on prayer, direct-giving, evangelistic services, combined with a cooler attitude to the jumble sales and whist drives, a bit disturbing. (John Collins once, light-heartedly and privately, suggested that I might speak to them on the text 'wist ye not', or else explain the doctrine of the last trump!) So a small group resolved not to let the Vicar have his own way this time, seeing this as the moment to stem the flowing tide of events. Spiritually, it was a crisis for the progress of St Mark's, and the staff gave themselves to prayer for a whole day beforehand. The meeting was a stormy one; John Collins was given heavenly wisdom, the treasurer over-stated his case, lost his supporters, and finally handing in his resignation he stormed out of the meeting, never to return to the church again. So, David arrived, to a room next-door to mine, in the vicarage. Perhaps significantly, he was introduced to the parochial ministry in this atmosphere of spiritual conflict in which he was later to be so frequently caught up.

Although the call of Christ had changed David's way of life from night-clubs to prayer-meetings, he was still in a congenial environment and among those of a similar background whilst he remained at Cambridge. God has a way of meeting us where we are, but he seldom has any intention of leaving us in the same place. To go to Gillingham was certainly to go somewhere different! David was suddenly jettisoned into a world of little back-to-back terraced houses, in a parish which had thirty-five pubs and a pickle factory. Everything was dominated by the Chatham dockyard, employing twelve thousand local inhabitants. The people were warm-hearted, with cockney humour, colourful language and great openness. There was no room for unrelated piety. People's needs and failings were not concealed behind a sophisticated veneer. Here, theology could be tested against the raw material of life, and truth had to be expressed with vivid illustration, practical application and a simple vocabulary. Nothing could be better than this setting for learning how to preach, and no one could have been better to learn from than John Collins. Children learn by copying their parents, and curates often do the same with their vicars. It used to be said of All Souls', Langham Place, in London, during the fifties, that on any Sunday you liked you could hear the famous rector, John Stott conducting the service, John Stott reading the lesson, John Stott leading the prayers, John Stott preaching, whilst John Stott was actually conducting a mission in Canada, having left all in the hands of his curates! To listen to some of David's early teaching at St Cuthbert's, York, is to hear the clear intonation, style and even sometimes illustrations of John Collins! Yet as his own style developed, he never lost that simplicity of expression, nor those personal anecdotes and dramatic illustrations. These, together with his careful choice of words, his fluency and the voice quality that led British Rail to employ him to record some of their platform announcements at York station, contributed to making him one of the most effective public speakers in the country.

A curate's stipend at that time was between £350 and £400 per year—a fairly meagre amount even in those pre-inflation days. So, buying a car was a daunting thing. Mine cost £60, was a 1936 Morris 8 with two doors and one flipper-indicator that worked. David's cost £80, was a 1938 model with four doors, two flippers and a sun-roof. Invited to lunch one day by a rather crusty older parishioner at the far end of the parish, we travelled there together in this vehicle. 'How did you come?' she asked abruptly, as she ushered us into her spick-and-span front room; 'by bus? or did you walk?' she said, peering at us like a curious sergeant-major. 'Well-er-actually, we came over in my car' explained David in a slightly anxious Wellingtonian accent. 'I see...' she rumbled disapprovingly, '...so you're the kind of curate who has a car, are you?' She was making us both feel like bloated capitalists being exposed by the pure party member from the Kremlin. She peered out through the window, obviously expecting a shining up-to-date sports model to be gracing the roadside; but the only car parked in the whole street was David's somewhat apologetic heap of pre-war Morris. 'Is that it?' she suddenly roared 'Is that it...? I thought you said you came by car.' She burst into peals of masculine laughter. Meanwhile, as David sat on the big mock-leather settee, grinning sheepishly and acknowledging that the ancient chariot was actually his, it became quite clear that he was 'in'. This was worthy of Gillingham. In pompous theological jargon it might have been called 'identification with the poor'; for David it was simply the natural consequence of following Christ. It was one of the early steps that led him along a road of considerable material hardship to fulfil his calling. A simple lifestyle was something he had spontaneously accepted long before he reached the point of articulating it in his preaching.

This course did not always meet with such warm approval either. On a day off in Eastbourne, that same car was greeted with unspoken but obvious scorn by a group of Cambridge friends, now on the way up in the business realm. Not to have a twentieth-century status symbol was in their eyes a mark of failure, and it hurt David. It is not very comfortable to find your own contemporaries regarding you as oddly religious and strangely unsuccessful. But then, crucifixion is not very comfortable.

Chatham, which with Rochester and Gillingham formed the conurbation called the Medway towns, had the highest juvenile delinquency rate in the country at that time. It was not altogether surprising. Many homes and parents were woefully inadequate. Moreover, apart from cinemas, dance-halls and bingo clubs there was no major youth centre. David and I often visited the billiard hall in the High Street, which fulfilled its traditional role of being the rallying point for small-time criminals and disaffected youth. We recruited from there for our own youth club, which was held in the rambling and dilapidated parish hall, a one-time primary school. From all that I knew of David, it seemed an unlikely place for him to feel at home. The 140 youngsters who turned up each week with their high-powered motor-cycles and leather jackets or their immaculate teddy-boy outfits, winkle-picker shoes and Elvis Presley hairstyles, could be as daunting as wild dervishes.

David took to the club like a reluctant duck to water. Protesting that this was not his scene, his warm bubbling humour and childlike delight in people made him as acceptable as he was accepting. Within weeks he was meeting every morning with an illiterate eighteen-year-old to teach a fresh verse of Scripture for each day. Mick, as he was called, was one of six boys who had been thrown out of the two-bedroom home by his parents at the age of fifteen, by which stage they reckoned he was capable of fending for himself. With sharpened rings on all his fingers, he had lived rough with a gang for a couple of years until he was invited to our club. There he discovered an unexpected soul-brother in David. Three or four weeks later, after a simple illustrated talk that David had given, Mick inarticulately took Christ for his saviour. It immediately became apparent that the church had no literature and few tried patterns for nurturing such young people. It was obvious too, that a strong community of love was vital to protect them against the destructive pressures in which they lived. Moreover, new ways of communicating had to be found for those whose reading never got beyond the pictures and headlines in the popular tabloids. Later David was to write 'in an age when people are satiated with words, various art forms can be immensely effective'; but already he was busy collecting Beaumont modern hymns such as 'Lord Jesus Christ, you have come to us'. Also there was a series of challenging dramatic sketches to display the world-wide mission of God, using newly minted words to familiar pop-songs, such as 'Does your chewing-gum lose its flavour on the bed-post over night?'. After all, the television jingles were already doing it, so why shouldn't he? What's more, it worked! It was a long way from the professionalism of the Riding Lights Theatre Company, and the use of songs and drama to turn the hearts of terrorists in Cromlyn Road jail, but the principles of evangelism were emerging out of daily experience.

So was the community of love at St Mark's. Nothing does more to expose foibles and to challenge idealism than the rough and tumble of sharing our lives with others. We wear masks to hide our real feelings: there is the mask of self-confidence or busyness or constant jokes. There is the 'Praise the Lord' mask and the mask of religious jargon. But the accepting fellowship which is realistically loving helps us to face our weakness and take off the mask. David had a streak of perfectionism in him and liked everything to be tidy and in order. This contributed to the rigour with which he insisted on high standards, accuracy of timing and quality in all aspects of Christian ministry. When preaching for him at one of the great evangelistic services in York Minster in the seventies, I saw the care with which the details of the service were arranged. Spontaneity was reckoned to be entirely compatible with detailed preparation. It was made quite clear, with beautiful tact, that I could not have a second more than twenty-two minutes to speak—unless of course I knew that I was obeying higher authority! But perfection itself is a sin, and contributes to depression. The Gillingham fellowship certainly didn't believe in it, and I might add, were in no danger of falling into it. They also were determined to pull David out of it. Rene and Judy, with their lively Cockney-style repartee, were leading mem-

bers of the youth fellowship and frequent uninvited
visitors to the Vicarage. They had a Nelson-like ability to
ignore the signals when it was time to go! 'Must you stay,
can't you go?' was one of the often repeated despairing
cries from David as the flow of light-hearted banter went
on and on, and they tried *again* to displace his beautifully
brushed wavy hair. 'Repeat the verse we learned yester-
day—James 1.2' said David on one occasion, trying to
turn the time-wasting in a more edifying direction. So
Rene began 'Count it all joy, my brothers'. She stopped
and scratched her head and then went on 'when you fall
into...various...various...er various' and she came to a
halt again. Then suddenly, *'Sins!'* she shouted triumph-
hantly. 'Count it all joy when you fall into various sins'
she repeated; while David, nonplussed and temporarily
speechless, half-angry and half-laughing eventually
blurted out 'No Rene, *temptations* or *trials,* not *sins!'*

Relationships seldom work out in a neat and tidy
fashion, nor can they always be kept to a strict timetable
of diary appointments. It never ceased to amaze me how
in the following years the Holy Spirit taught David such
patience when his carefully ordered arrangements were
disrupted by the human factor. But there was an ever-
deepening awareness as his ministry went on, that relationships between people had to come second only to the
relationship with Christ. Truth in relationships was even
more important than truth in doctrine. Forgiveness and
reconciliation became major themes of his preaching,
sometimes leading to a startling response from the congregation. After a celebration evening in Truro, there
were queues outside the telephone boxes as those
touched by the Spirit sought to put things right with
neighbours, relatives, or friends. But there was an angry
reaction at the Nottingham Evangelical Conference in
1977 when he boldly applied the same lesson over Pro-

testant attitudes to Roman Catholics. David had confided in me very soon after he had arrived at the Vicarage at Gillingham, that he had made 1 Corinthians 13 a subject of daily meditation the previous year, and was intending to continue to do so while at St Mark's. I was aware that there was a continuing radical reappraisal going on within him about what the love of Christ actually means in practical day-to-day living.

There were two areas where David did not attempt to conceal his ignorance during that period: he did not understand women or children. It was not that he didn't enjoy the company of the opposite sex, it was just that he didn't quite know how they fitted into the male scheme of things! Of course this didn't appear to matter greatly as we both regarded ourselves as safe bachelors. In one way it wasn't surprising. We had both been brought up in the masculine environment of a single-sex independent school. When I arrived at St Mark's, the youth club consisted of sixteen girls and one or two very brave young men. It appeared much more desirable to win the elusive males for Christ, especially as they were the only ones in our thinking at that time who could eventually be entrusted with leadership. The cultural environment from which we both came had impressed on us an unconscious arrogance, and although this was challenged with a delightful openness and frankness by the women and girls in the parish (as well as by Diana Collins, the gifted and glamorous wife of our Vicar), our shining armour was only mildly dented. Moreover, our inherited understanding of the role of men appeared to us to be reinforced by Bible teaching. It is no wonder that it took a long time before women were accepted into the leadership at St Michael-le-Belfrey. Meanwhile we sailed unscathed through our Gillingham days. While working at St Helen's, Bishopsgate in London, I had a somewhat whirlwind romance, and got engaged in the New Year of 1964. Out of loyalty to David, I took my very attractive fiancée, Clare, up to Cambridge to meet him. By then, he was on the staff of the Round Church. He was visibly shaken by my news, but in a delightful way he asked, 'Where on earth did you manage to find her?' as if I had stumbled on some exclusive boutique offering quality goods at greatly reduced prices. He then went on to admit that Paul's exhortation in 1 Corinthians 7 had been losing its hold upon him, and he gravely doubted whether the gift of celibacy had been bestowed upon him. So I was not a bit surprised to get the ecstatic news soon afterwards of his secret engagement to Anne. Her strength of character, poetic sensitivity and exceptional visionary gifts, brought into being a combined ministry through which the Spirit was to reach out round the world. But their deep and lovely relationship was to be developed through inevitable pain and suffering. It was impossible for two such people to come together without sparks of friction as well as profound affection. Yet David discovered in Anne a person who, under God, could sweep away the stilted chauvinism of his youth and open a whole new world of the rich partnership to be found between men and women.

The thrill of evangelism, the vision for the church, the complex insecurities which plagued him, his capacity for work and his difficulty in relaxing, all militated against his giving to Anne the time that she deserved; but God gave her grace and the church in York owes so much to her ministry. From David there flowed a river of books, tapes, videos, University missions, and celebrations in towns and cities around the world, all providing inspiration to the witness of a flagging church. Ministers were revived, unbelievers convinced, leaders trained, new patterns and emphases proclaimed.

Perhaps a good many bachelors in the mid-twenties find young children rather irritating and strange creatures. David certainly did. As far as he was concerned they had sniffling noses, silly voices and simply got in the way. I suspect he would have gladly evaded any responsibility for them. It was quite plain to me that he was greatly relieved when I was put in charge of the Sunday School, whilst he was left manfully struggling with the eleven to fourteen year-old boys in the Pathfinder group. But John Collins, amongst his other skills in ministry, was a gifted communicator to children, and quickly introduced a monthly family service. There he captured the attention of all from the four-year-olds to the octogenarians, using visual aids and whimsical humour to give clear biblical teaching. David was captivated by this too, and began to turn his attention to developing similar gifts.

From a preaching angle alone, this was formative. To find ways of conveying great truths with simple words and clarity, so that a child can understand, is a vital discipline. Spiritual truth is not easy to grasp. We struggle to see and take in what God is saying. 'Any fool can make simple things complicated,' said Charles Simeon, 'but the wise preacher makes difficult things plain.' In the end it is only by the action of the Holy Spirit that we see truth at all, but simplicity opens the door to him. Family services became a major feature of David's ministry as the years went on, and a source of understanding for many. I remember attending a service at St Cuthbert's soon after he had moved into the parish. There were a good number in the tiny church, and David was expounding the story of Jericho. He had gone to town (so to speak!) with his visual aid, and on the chancel steps stood the towering walls of Jericho precariously built of cardboard. It was dramatic. It was unforgettable. I am sure that no child or adult could have failed to see the lesson of faith that was being unfolded. David afterwards confessed to me that there was one major discrepancy between his illustration and the biblical story. 'It required faith to keep my walls *up,* not bring them *down*', he said.

Perhaps the encounter with children contributed to the growth of one of the most attractive and challenging features of his life, which was his unashamed faith. He really believed God. There was nothing naive or simplistic about this, and over the years his confidence was tested by depression, illness, painful experiences and tough circumstances. At the root of this faith was the certainty that God had called him and that he was never going to go back on that call. I can't believe that anything else would have taken him to Gillingham; nor could anything else have sustained him through the difficult times of severe bronchial asthma and the pressure of a pathetically low stipend. I remember his describing to me a number of petty irritations to which he was being subjected after a number of years at St Cuthbert's when the work was growing and his considerable ability was plain. 'You know, David,' he said, 'I am still only a curate—and treated like it!' But he learned to submit, in faith.

A few weeks before he died, we had been laughing together about a video tape of one of his lectures that I had seen in the USA. It had been prefaced with a rather pompous introduction which spoke of 'the men God has raised up over the centuries—Martin Luther, John Wesley, Billy Graham...and now David Watson!'. We chortled about this, but he was actually rather depressed by it, as well as amused. We went to on to discuss the effects of his ministry, and the number of people who had been touched through books, talks, celebrations and broadcasts. It was then that he said, in a way that I suppose many who have found themselves being used by

God could echo, 'I really don't understand why this should happen to me? Why have I been given this position?' That is the key thing in faith. There is *no* explanation why God should use someone. It is not discipline, determination, energy, eloquence, personality or ability that matter in the end, useful though all these may be. It is that God has chosen us 'for good works which he has prepared beforehand for us to walk in'. And David walked in these with childlike amazement. This is the joy of responding to a call, and it leaves a person with no sense of achievement about faith. After all, what else can you do but trust a God who has come to you, confided in you, and given you his work to do.

It was during the final year that I was with him at Gillingham, that something fresh began to happen in his life and ministry. It is always difficult to describe spiritual changes that you think you see in another person. All I can say is that it was something like a car engine, which because of cold or damp, has been firing on only three cylinders, and suddenly begins to get bursts of full acceleration. His preaching, his counselling, his personal life began to have sparks of a different quality. He knew it himself, but didn't fully understand why. In fact, he had been spending some time on St Paul's teaching in Romans 6, which is a passage central to Christian discipleship, but not easy to grasp in experience. The truth that we have died with Christ and are risen with him, is frequently stated as a fact for the believer and it is at the heart of the symbolism of baptism. But what does it actually mean when you are fiercely tempted to be lazy, greedy, irritable or self-seeking? How does it relate to everyday living? This is what David wrestled with in his teaching and I remember him vainly using an illustration about the corpse of an alcoholic. 'Now that he is dead, the whisky bottle no longer has any power over him. You can wave it under his nose but he doesn't respond,' he explained. The reaction was one of vocal protest. The youth club were not dead dossers; they were vigorously alive, and attracted like magnets to a whole range of sins! But they couldn't help being intrigued by David's obvious conviction and the real change that had taken place in him. Interest grew into longing, and longing into heart-searching. As with so many of the great truths about Christ and the Cross, the intellect gets out of its depth; it can go so far, but then has to cry out to the Holy Spirit for understanding. This was what David had been discovering, and (as so often in later years) he led others along the path that God seemed to be opening up ahead of him, even though he didn't know where it would end. It was while he was doing this, that there came that revelation which can only be given by the Spirit. He knew that he was one with Jesus, and that in that relationship he possessed a new power to die to pride and self-seeking and live for what is right. It was a fresh dimension of faith, and it had the effect of stimulating others. It played an important part in the renewal of the whole of St Mark's at that stage. It was also a vital preparation for the filling of the Spirit and the exercise of gifts which were to come later. To discover what it means to be united in Christ's death and resurrection was something that David always urged on those who were seeking the power of the Spirit.

Here again, one of the facets of Christian leadership can be seen. A man of faith who can expose his difficulties and doubts side-by-side with his longing to know God and certainty that Christ is reliable, will stimulate others without haranguing them. On one occasion when he was preaching on a passage in Matthew 6, which deals with anxiety, he confessed that he had not been able to over-come certain worries himself, though he knew that the teaching of Jesus was true. A workman said afterwards, 'I found that sermon convinced me about what he was saying, more than any other that I have ever heard'. It was sometimes an uncomfortable honesty that he had, but it made him easy to identify with and it made the promise of Christ accessible to ordinary people. In 1981 when he was leading a celebration in Birmingham, he was interviewed by ATV. One of the cameramen admitted afterwards that he found David almost too open about his marriage and his depressions. 'What he said came too near the bone for my liking,' he commented.

In 1961 I left Gillingham and went to London; a few months later David went to Cambridge. We kept in touch over the years, acting as best man at each other's weddings. In 1970, it looked as if we might work together again. Things were very difficult at St Cuthbert's, and David was wondering about a move. The then Provost of Birmingham Cathedral, Bishop Sinker, warmed to the idea of his coming on to the staff. I fixed a date with him, and we arranged to meet at New Street station. What I foolishly had not reckoned on were the extensive building operations being done by British Rail, which meant that there were two entrances instead of one. The inevitable happened. I went to the one and he to the other. I vainly searched the surging body of passengers; he waited with mounting annoyance for someone to collect him. Somehow, incredible though it may seem, by changing our positions we succeeded in missing each other for the next three hours! In despair, David eventually caught a train back to York—to begin the most fruitful part of his ministry there, and the work which brought people from all over the world to learn about the meaning of renewal in the Church. I wish that I could say with a clear conscience that it was the Lord who frustrated our plans that day. It would cover up my bungling. I am afraid that there was rather too much human error there to claim divine intervention. But he certainly did use the frustration and waste of time to speak to us both. Many Christian leaders attempt to move out of a vital work to which God has called them just before the important stage begins. And while I am sure there are other ways in which God might have spoken to David, he used that ridiculous incident to confirm that York was the place in which he was to stay.

On Saturday, 8th January 1983 Teddy Saunders telephoned me from St Michael's Chester Square in London. 'I've got some bad news, I'm afraid' he said. 'David Watson has got to have a major operation next Tuesday. The consultant has diagnosed a malignant ulcer and is going to act swiftly. He wondered whether you would be willing to undertake at short notice the lecture course which he is due to take at Fuller Seminary. I have got him here with me at the moment, and he would love to have a word with you.' David came on, his cheery relaxed voice belying the turmoil that must have been there, and told me more of the situation. I replied that I would do my best to take on some of the lectures if I could get free of one or two engagements in my diary. We went on to talk of the shock of the doctor's discovery and what it was going to mean for him. 'The consultant is very hopeful,' he said. 'The only problem is that I shall probably have to have a colostomy. It is likely to mean cutting down on the travelling, but otherwise I shall be able to continue all right.'

I came away from the conversation stunned and with a sense of being strangely challenged. Just a week or two before Christmas I had been with him at a conference for Christian leaders, and he had been on such good form. I could scarcely believe that so soon afterwards, there was the threat of death hanging over him. There was something deeper than that too. It was as if the Lord was saying to me, 'I am asking David to put his life in my hands in a completely new way. He has already surrendered his energy and gifts and time, but now I am asking a new thing. It is that he be willing to surrender even his physical being for my sake and the gospel.' I became aware at that moment not only of the immense privilege we are given of belonging completely to the Lord but also of the price that has to be paid. It means being willing to give everything, even life itself. I realised that David was ready for the further step, but now my own life was also being opened up to the searching gaze of God. There is nothing that focuses the issue of life so clearly as death. I became acutely aware that there were so many desires and attitudes in my heart that were completely wrong. I found a strange longing to change direction and be filled afresh with the spirit of Christ. Real repentance is a strangely refreshing and releasing gift of God. It is not just something for the beginning of our discipleship. It is a way of life.

From that morning onwards, I had an inner sense that David was going to die, although like many others I hoped and prayed and at times sincerely felt that this was not going to be so. It seemed to me that God was showing me afresh that, as with the martyrs, God has chosen to use the deaths of some of his servants as an integral part of their ministry. Death for a believer is not a tragedy nor is it a victory for the evil one. It is in so many ways the ultimate act of faith, when we let go of everything that we have and commit our body, mind and soul into the hands of the Saviour, in sure and certain hope of the resurrection from the dead. It is that act of faith that makes the powers of darkness tremble, even more than when they see the signs and wonders that follow from the power of the gospel.

The final year of David's life and ministry was a very remarkable one. He had already become widely known and recognised in the Church in this country as well as in Scandinavia, the USA, South Africa, Australia, New Zealand and other places. His sixty or so university missions had affected a whole generation of students. In St Michael-le-Belfrey, York, pioneer work had been done to show how the Holy Spirit can take a congregation forward both in depth of worship and growth in numbers. The value of drama and dance for evangelism had been demonstrated. In addition, an astonishing seventeen books had poured from his pen, giving permanence to his preaching. Thousands had come to faith through him, and many more had been encouraged and built up in their Christian lives. So the announcement of his cancer sent shock-waves to many parts of the world. It was a new test for him and a new opportunity, too.

One principle of evangelism which he recognised early on was that the gospel must be embodied as well as preached. It is not enough simply to share the good news, it has to be shown in practical situations, both corporately and personally. What is the gospel to a person who has just been told he has cancer? David could have withdrawn from public life at this point to struggle with the answer to that in the privacy of his home and with a few friends. Instead, he chose to share his life even more widely and publicly than before, and continued to allow truths to be worked out in his own body.

On Tuesday, 19th April 1983, he spoke to Nick Page on BBC radio. With characteristic honesty, he described his dismay and his discomfort at the news of the disease. He then went on to pose the issues of faith which were to provoke thousands, and were to occupy much of his thinking during those final months. The first was this: How do we stand up to the dread that surrounds the single word 'cancer' in this day and age? Words that may sound trivial in the bloom of health, become electrifying when spoken out of real suffering. So David arrested listeners when he said:

'If he doesn't heal me, then I have to face a mystery. God does have a purpose in our lives, and his purpose through us is not measured by the length of our life; therefore if God takes me to be with himself now or in a year's time then I hope I have the confidence that he has done the work which he wants to do through me and that I can really enjoy heaven.'

But the second issue is this. How far do we expect God to heal such things as terminal cancer? David answered:

'Now at this moment, I have very peaceful and settled faith that there is healing. I may be wrong, but that is what I believe. I have felt the power of God in my body to heal. I have heard prophetic words from the Lord that he is going to heal. I have put all that together and say, yes, I think he is doing it.'

By saying these things he put himself at risk. There were going to be those watching his progress to see whether his confidence would hold up if death became a reality. There were also those who felt that what happened to him would be the acid test of whether the healing ministry is for today, at all. I heard a reporter from one of the national daily papers say 'He has claimed on the radio that he is healed. Let's wait and see'. In fact, David had given a more balanced comment than many superficial listeners had heard. When Nick Page pressed him about his healing, he replied:

'If I found it was not coming, and it was perfectly clear from later scans in the forthcoming months that I am not being

34

healed, I hope I have got to the position of real trust in him, to know that the best is yet to be. You know, actually to be with Christ and free from pain and suffering, tears and all the problems and injustices of this world, there is nothing more glorious than that; that is why I am genuinely at the place where I really want to be in heaven'.

As he regained strength that summer and began to fill his diary as full as it had ever been for the autumn, hopes were raised afresh. He spoke with the authority of a 'dying man' to 'dying men', and at the Defence Ministry, the Arts Centre, the Commons and the Lords, and other places, there was an unusual quality of power in his words. He emphasised particularly the promise that signs and wonders follow the proclamation of the gospel. One person was healed of cancer while listening to the broadcast in April. Many others experienced the power of God through his ministry during the latter part of the year.

It was not until late November and December that it became clear that the cancer had grown considerably in his liver. Even until just before Christmas, he was still hoping to be able to fulfil a lecture series at Fuller Seminary in the USA, but others could see that travel was out of the question. He continued to struggle in his own heart over the healing of his body, which did not appear to be coming. It was a dialogue with his Lord in which he expressed the agony of his dilemma and yet paradoxically was at peace.

The announcement of his death came as a profound shock to many. The thousands who had been stimulated to pray for him were stunned and unable to believe that he had not been healed. I found the question being flung at me, 'What about all these Christians who had been praying for his healing? Were they wrong?' A succession of answers came flooding into my mind. Look how many people have begun to learn to pray. It is often the crisis which brings us to our knees. It is not until we find ourselves unable to do anything in our own strength that we turn to Christ, and that is how he draws us to himself. It was the suffering of David that made many pray. Look how many people have been brought together. There is a wonderful sense of unity in a common love and a common cause. This is what his illness had done. Look how many have been challenged. In David, God had focused so many eyes on to the fear that is rife in our society. It was as if God had taken the word 'cancer', written it over his life, and said, 'Are you afraid of it?' David had replied, 'Yes I am, but I am going to find out from Christ how he wants me to conquer it.'

His book *Fear No Evil* is the product of that victory. Look how many people are being matured. Death has a way of exposing us. No doubt some have been offended by it. It will have confirmed their doubts. They did not really believe in healing. They hoped a bit, and waited at a distance and now their scepticism has been proved justified in their own eyes. God doesn't defend himself against sceptics; he looks for ways of touching their hearts. Some will be introverted. For them David's death has come as a threat; it means that even those who trust Christ implicitly are not insured against the agonies of life. If it could happen to him, it could happen to anyone. They can't see the glory that comes in suffering. Some have been confused. They have put their heart and soul into believing and now in the bold attempt to commit themselves to the promises of God, they seem to have been terribly let down. Was that how Mary and Martha felt when Jesus did not arrive in time to heal Lazarus, and his body was already mouldering in the grave? If so, why wasn't David raised from the dead, like Lazarus? It seems to me that with Lazarus, Jesus was preparing the people for his own resurrection, but now he is risen. We know it, and that is how we know that David is more alive than ever before.

What had the Lord been doing then? Certainly not denying healing. I have seen cancer patients healed. I am sure we have yet to see what happens when people really trust him to reveal himself. The kingdom of God is not just a dispensary for the sick; it is much bigger than that. What is more, we only have a foretaste now; the day when there is no more sickness, disease, tears, or pain is yet to come. When Timothy suffered from tummy problems and Epaphroditus nearly died, the apostle Paul did not get up-tight saying that it was all because of lack of faith. What has happened certainly does not deny healing, but just puts it in its place.

What *has* the Lord been doing then? Certainly not denying the rule of God. Someone said to me, 'I suppose his ministry is finished now'. I could see the implication in what he was saying. He meant 'of course it's not the best, but we can rejoice in the fact that he is in heaven. However, what a shame! What a lot he might have accomplished if he had lived his full span!' In other words, death has taken over from God, and disease really has got the upper hand. Perhaps God will eventually get the final victory, but at the moment the other side is winning. To this there must be a resounding 'NO!' So the question rears its head again. *Why then did he die?* It is fascinating that questions like this are so intertwined with the person of Jesus Christ. Why should a young man in the prime of his life, with an unparalleled character and whose ministry had surpassed all who had ever lived before him, die an agonising death at the age of thirty-three? The answer is that he has shown us the nature of death. It is no longer a tyrant to be feared, but to those who have put their faith in him it is the old family servant who opens the door of the house to welcome the children home. It was like that for David as he stepped into heaven. It has shown us the nature of our ministry, too. Was Christ's death the end of his work? Again a resounding 'NO' rings out. The secret of the power of Christ is always to be found in our human weakness, and there is no point at which we are weaker than when we die. David's ministry will continue because it was the ministry of the Spirit of Christ.

Chapter Two

LIVING
IN COMMUNITY

by

Andrew Maries

Andrew Maries began his association with David
Watson's ministry during the early days at St Cuthbert's.
For six years he lived in the rectory household with the
Watson family. He is a pioneer in balancing old and new
styles in church music, and is the Director of Music at St
Michael-le-Belfrey.

I first met David Watson in 1968 whilst I was a music student at York University. A friend of mine was asked to play his violin in a special guest service at the little church of St Cuthbert's and I offered him a lift. It was an exciting service and the lively singing and clear committed preaching impressed me greatly. I knew nothing of the man or the church and never imagined that my chance visit would begin a long association with both which has changed the pattern of my life.

David was an awesome figure, particularly in clerical garb, and in those early days I felt very nervous even of speaking to him. He had an impressive gift of remembering your name, but even so I felt I could never get really close to him or penetrate those inscrutable eyes. His was the image of the typical Anglican evangelical preacher: clipped speech, public school background, immaculate in dress and manners. As such he occupied a pedestal in most people's minds, but he kept his private life to himself.

David, Anne and their two children Fiona and Guy lived in the Rectory, a huge rambling establishment. The one mass invasion of their privacy occurred once a week when the parish fellowship meeting was held in the front office. It started out with only a few but by the time I arrived numbers had grown so much that sound relays were used, first next door in the study and soon all over the house in lounges and attic bedrooms. You had to get there early otherwise you didn't get a seat in the main room.

David had one particular fan club—a group of old ladies who always installed themselves in the front row. They all wore funny hats and punctuated the meetings with 'Amens' and 'Hallelujahs' and a strange religious jargon from a bygone age, quite foreign to me. We students were often secretly amused by such phrases as 'O Lord we lift so-and-so's leg up before thee' or 'O Lord, thou art the Great Undertaker'. But these characters were the pillars of those early days and all of us were caught up in the excitement of the beginning of a new work of God.

We lapped up the teaching David gave as he worked systematically through a New Testament Epistle explaining and illustrating each verse and applying them to ordinary life and experience. Despite the invasion of their home, I hardly ever met Anne or the children at that time. They would retreat into the bedroom before the multitudes arrived and re-emerge when we had all left. It wasn't until later that I began to understand some of the immense pressures David's public ministry imposed on the domestic front.

It was also some time before I came to appreciate some of the paradoxes of David's character. In public he was a powerful communicator with a brilliant mind, a great leader and enabler of others. In private, he was vulnerable to depression and self-doubt, often acutely sensitive to what others thought of him. He frequently buried himself in his work, sometimes to avoid facing up to himself and often to the cost of his family.

His preaching and teaching were masterful in their clear and logical structure, their use of humour and illustration. It was amazing how he would always be coming up with new anecdotes, jokes and telling quotations. He had a vast filing system and knew exactly when and where he had last used a particular illustration. He knew how to handle an audience and how to keep them hanging on his every word, using tension and relaxation like a great actor. These skills did not come easily to him; he had to learn his trade the hard way, endlessly honing and perfecting the structure and presentation of his teaching. But whatever the theme or Scripture he expounded, whatever the intellectual level of his hearers, his approach was always the same: profoundly simple, crystal clear and challengingly direct.

These superb gifts aided tremendously the developing and maturing of the congregation at St Cuthbert's. The weekly expounding of the Scriptures and their earthing in practical daily living rooted the renewal in fertile ground, and people grew in faith and commitment. The church began to discover itself as the Body of Christ: a corporate, responsible, dynamic organism of which each member was a vital part. David's own involvement in the charismatic movement brought a new free and expressive style of worship to our fellowship, although it was some years before this could be integrated into public worship. Under these influences David himself became more relaxed and open. He had an earnest desire to encourage growth and maturity in others and soon elders were created to share the burgeoning ministry under his influence and direction.

Numbers continued to grow and in 1973 the congregation moved into the larger church of St Michael-le-Belfrey, next to York Minster. This coincided with my own return to York. After leaving university I worked for

a year under Michael Harper in the London office of the
Fountain Trust where I came across Graham Pulkingham
and the Church of the Redeemer at Houston, Texas. I
was attracted by the concept of 'community' and when I
returned to York to become organist was most interested
to find people there also talking about it. Six months later
I moved into a pioneer household in the Rectory. I have
to admit to slightly selfish motives of getting my washing
done for me, but I unwittingly embarked upon one of the
most significant and formative experiences of my life.
This lasted for six years.

Who would have guessed that I would end up living
closely with a man that I had at first found so stiff and
awesome! We owed this uncomfortable mix to Anne
Watson. Both she and David had a great vision for the
place and significance of worship (and to this I owe my
present ministry), but Anne particularly had a vision for
community. Behind any great man there is usually an
equally great woman and whilst David has been the
communicator and interpreter, Anne has been the insti-
gator and visionary. Like Aaron and Moses they have
complemented each other in a remarkable way. Of the
things which St Michael's has been known for: the
music and worship, the banners, the dance, the children's
work, the shop, even the concept of shared leadership
and women's ministry; most were spawned from her
vision which she then devoted herself to fulfilling. The
household came into existence through her perseverance,
despite considerable resistance. It's doubtful whether
David would have naturally entered into something so
potentially disruptive to his well organised routine!

I arrived on a Saturday morning with cases, boxes and
an upright piano, just as the elders emerged from David's
study after an early-morning prayer-meeting. It was not a
very opportune moment. They were none too pleased

about this strange community experiment, nor were they keen to manoeuvre an extremely heavy piano round a very awkward corner, doing a somersault with it in the process, so that it would go in the back living-room! I soon got the impression that this and other invitations really came from Anne, together with another girl who acted as perpetrator and who constantly performed what she called 'the ministry of knocking off rough edges'. This usually meant mercilessly pushing David into situations or relations which he would naturally have rather avoided. I know he didn't get on with me at first, I read it in his book! He never expressed it at the time, and in fact one often wondered what he was really feeling or thinking. I didn't get on with him either; his 'big daddy' approach in those early days made us all react like naughty children. We often did things as a protest against his stiff and starchy manner!

Community living meant lots of trauma, but also lots of fun! For us, most of this went on behind the glass door which separated the office and study from the rest of the house. David would sit securely at his desk in the calm and ordered world of sermon preparation and interviews while the rest of us got on with the ups and downs of living together amid the chaos of children, cats, dogs and junk furniture which benevolent parishioners were always dumping on us. David might make the occasional foray for food or coffee to find heavy counselling in session on the settee, but would quickly retreat to the sanctity of the study.

Looking back, there were several amusing incidents. One such event occurred over the green paint I found in the 'workshop', a dirty little glory-hole under the stairs. There wasn't a label on the tin and when I opened it up I found it was some ex-army green gloss. We had just had the chimney-sweep in the breakfast-room and, as it was all looking rather dowdy, we decided to embark on an immediate improvement scheme with the green paint. Anne was away at the time, with the children, and David was incarcerated in the study as usual. I was up a ladder and we were half-way through our grand transformation when the door opened... *Oh dear!* He didn't like it. The eyebrows knitted and a few clipped reproofs withered our enthusiasm. The well-organised routine had been disrupted. Apart from the fact that he disliked green as a colour and was suffering from asthma as a result of the paint fumes, some university students were coming to tea. Where were they going to have it now!? The only place left was the office. We had a most embarrassing and self-conscious tea amid the duplicators and typewriters and it took some time before the lingering aroma of paint and fried onions was banished from the front rooms.

Some time later, in our 'back to nature' period, Anne and I decided to create a vegetable garden on part of the enormous bottom lawn. I hired a rotavator and set about digging up the grass. It was great fun! Unfortunately David did not share our 'digging for survival' vision and when he eventually came down to inspect what was going on it was too late. He had a job to hide his horror when he saw what had happened to his beautiful lawn. We grew vegetables for a few years and I even began to build a greenhouse out of enormous numbers of half sash-windows which I'd got 'cheap'. It remained unfinished as a testament to my folly and became a standing joke until another member of the community later demolished it with a sledgehammer! David meanwhile kept well out of the way. He actually hated gardening!

Gradually, David began to be more integrated into household life. Chinks began to appear in his armour and he began to make himself more vulnerable to the rest of us. He still appeared at early-morning prayers fully dressed and bang on time while the rest of us staggered down late, bleary-eyed and still in our pyjamas, but he was a softer David, more accepting. Though so different in character we achieved over the years a deep love and unity that transcended our tastes and preferences, even our differences in age. We became 'family' and that bond continued. How often we commiserated with each other as we humped the same heavy wardrobe up and down the narrow stairs as community members swopped bedrooms in an endless ballet. How often we watched David dissolve into helpless giggles over some household *faux-pas* or saw him broken and vulnerable in the midst of a particularly traumatic crisis.

Part of the household's function was to support the ministry—including David's mission work and my own provision of the music and worship of the church. As households spread there were at one time thirty or forty people working within the church or on David's team. Through the experience of living closer together and sharing life on a more basic level, we all learnt much about ourselves and about our Christianity. Everyone matured significantly through their time spent in the household, and the themes of love, acceptance and commitment, of which we read in the New Testament, took on fresh and immediate meaning. The ethos of community continues to affect deeply the whole life, ministry and worship of St Michael's. Whilst many households did not survive, mainly because they lacked clear direction through the difficulties, 'community' and the relationships built up at that time still form the backbone of the church.

David's new insights, gained from our experience together, gave his preaching and teaching a powerful and prophetic edge, which the wider Church flocked to hear. He was able to teach about a radical commitment to Christ, about shared leadership, simple lifestyle, the creative arts, renewed worship, and then to say 'Come and see!'

The move to St Michael's profoundly affected the ministry of the church; we became more public, more accessible to the many visitors to York. The graceful architecture of the church and its surroundings affected our worship, lending it dignity and sensitivity. We began to marry tradition and informality, structure and spontaneity, and our message of renewal began to speak to many other traditions. Renewal Weeks started and hundreds of clergy and lay leaders began to share the life and ministry we were developing by coming to stay with us in the homes of church members.

We also went out from the church. David had done a few missions with help from the Fisherfolk, a travelling group of musicians from the Redeemer church in Houston whose ministry of leading worship sprang from their community lifestyle. David began to see the power of this corporate ministry in that it reflected the corporate nature of the Body of Christ. If we loved one another, God's presence would be experienced among us and the power of the gospel released. He determined to form such a group from the fellowship of St Michael's who could take with them something of the quality of life and ministry which we shared in York. He drew his team from household members, the music group and helpers in the 'Mustard Seed', the church-based shop.

The team had humble beginnings. Our first engagement was in a small Town Hall near York for an evening renewal meeting. I, and my friend Phil who shared the leadership of the music group with me, decided we'd get the congregation to do a round. We duly divided them into two halves, one to follow me, the other Phil. After we had started I began to feel a reddening of the cheeks and a warming of the ears as I gradually realised that we had forgotten to organise which half was doing the canon. Of course we ended up singing exactly the same all the way through while David shifted uncomfortably in the front row and tried not to meet our eyes! He was so patient. His vision for corporate ministry made him stick to his guns in the face of many a mission committee who, having invited him, found that he wouldn't come without his team.

We gradually improved and eventually became proficient in handling large numbers of people more professionally and leading them in worship and praise. We also took seminars to teach and explain the various aspects of our church life back at home. I'm sure it gladdened David's heart to see those so much younger and more inexperienced than himself mature and develop our various ministries. We were able to encourage him as well. Many times we gave support as he wrestled with doubts and uncertainties over talks he had prepared, or periods of deep depression when he felt he had not done his best in presenting the message and that people had not responded as he'd hoped.

He was a hard man to keep up with. He would often organise punishing schedules and then wonder why we were falling apart with exhaustion, especially since we had comparatively little to do while he spent every spare moment preparing and polishing his talks. I remember in the Dublin mission having half an hour off in a whole week. It was just time to rush off to see the Book of Kells and rush back again for the next event! Sometimes, in reaction to the pressure, we would dissolve into hysterics —especially when the drama group Riding Lights were with us. David would emerge from the isolation of sermon preparation slightly irritated that we could enjoy ourselves while he missed all the fun. The generation gap was always a bit of a problem, particularly as he often found it so hard to relax and let himself go.

It was a remarkable thing that people of such diverse age-groups and cultural backgrounds could achieve such a measure of oneness together. In our prayer times before the meetings we would link arms and pray for one another and the forthcoming meeting. Sometimes David would go into the middle and we would lay hands on him and minister to him, praying that God might lift a depression, heal a sore throat or give him power and authority in his preaching. It was an exciting time for all of us, and such a great privilege to visit places as far apart as Truro and Newcastle, Belfast and Sheffield, sharing with them some of the insights we were experiencing as a church.

In later years David's ministry to the wider Church evolved into a threefold call to evangelism, renewal and reconciliation. His gifts, his background and his experience gave him an unrivalled position as one acceptable to many churches and many traditions. With his team (now full-time in London and newly recruited for the purpose) he was able to live out and express his teaching, which brought together Catholics, Anglicans, Pentecostals, Methodists and others in great city festivals. Of all the themes he took, reconciliation was perhaps the most telling and this aspect of his ministry will be very greatly missed. Commitment to Christ must be personal, but it must also renew structures and relationships. He often called the divisions between the churches the 'cancer' of the Body of Christ, and it is ironic that cancer should have eventually attacked his own body.

The move to London caused David, Anne and their family to suffer great trauma and grief, especially in the first months. For all of us who had formed such deep relationships with them over the years, the parting was full of pain. They said that they experienced a death when they left us. This was true for many of us too, although we still had the warmth of our own fellowship to fall back on. There is no doubt of the rightness of the move for the growth and maturity of our own church here in York, but it has been harder to understand God's purposes for the Watsons. We needed to find our own identity apart from David and Anne, and it was a decision of great courage and discernment on their part to make the break. One can only wonder at the mystery of God's plan for them. When they arrived David's ministry began to change: the big mission events seemed to be less appropriate, his teaching, so rooted in a local church situation, suffered from the lack of a satisfactory base, the illness struck him like a thunderbolt. Certainly a superstitious person would have advised against the writing of one's autobiography so comparatively early in life, especially when the last page discloses the recent discovery of terminal cancer!

I still feel confused about it all. Why did he die? I haven't yet felt an inclination to read his last book *Fear No Evil* because he writes at least part of it in the belief that he will be healed. It saddened me that David plunged frantically back into his work almost as soon as he got out of the hospital bed. It was as if the healing element gave him an excuse to carry on just as before. How I regret that David never consistently heeded the warnings of doctors and friends to slow down and get out of the spiral of work and pressure in which he was trapped. Some of us felt that his identity and sense of self-worth was so tied up in his ministry that he just didn't know what to do without it. I was encouraged that at the very end, he had discovered what he knew in his mind but found so difficult to translate in his heart: that God wanted to own him, without all the striving and activity, and that he wanted to show David a father's love and security which he had so sadly lacked in his own childhood. I don't think God let him down by not healing him and I certainly don't think we should desperately scratch around to find reasons to prop up our own faith. It is a mystery and we can only rejoice that he found peace and tranquillity of spirit at the last.

What an enormous debt I owe to both David and Anne for the sacrifices they made to enable me to enter my own ministry of music and worship. Like many others, I have so much cause to thank God that he brought them across my path. Their initial obedience to God and to the vision he gave them has produced such an abundance of fruit in thousands of lives all over the world. And the ministry continues. The books and tapes will remain foundational teaching aids of so many aspects of Christian life and ministry. And there is one abiding living memorial in the continuing development of the Body of Christ at St Michael-le-Belfrey, York—a letter of recommendation written on tablets of human hearts.

Chapter Three

THE RECONCILER

by

Michael Harper

Michael Harper is an Anglican minister and the International Director of SOMA (Sharing of Ministries Abroad), and was for many years the Editor of *Renewal* magazine. He is the author of twelve books and lives in Sussex.

'He's the only one who can bring us all together' was the Rev Donald English's comment to me about David Watson when we were talking during 1983. This ability to reconcile was surely one of David's greatest qualities. It had nothing to do with having a magnetic personality, nor with skill at ecumenical diplomacy, and certainly not with compromising or watering down the gospel to suit all tastes, which David never did. Douglas Greenfield, who for a number of years co-ordinated David's extensive travelling ministry, described him as a man 'full of love'. It was that which drew such a wide cross-section of Christian leaders to support and work together for the missions and festivals of praise he held all over Britain, and later the world.

I first met David in Cambridge in the rooms of a student at Selwyn College. David was then at Ridley Hall preparing for Anglican ordination. I had just moved to All Souls', Langham Place and I remember talking with him about his own future. From those early days it was clear to many of us that he had a distinguished career ahead of him. I don't think this possibility occurred to him at all, and my earliest impressions were of a humble man whose only concern was the glory of God and serving the poor. He was not the least bit interested in going to a prestigious parish (he was invited by John Stott to go to All Souls') and told me he wanted to work with working-class people; his first appointment was in Gillingham, Kent.

It was in that parish that the charismatic renewal first surfaced in the Church of England.

He then moved to the Round Church in Cambridge and I saw him more frequently as the charismatic renewal gathered momentum in Britain. We were involved (with John Collins and David MacInnes) in an interesting dialogue with Dr Martyn Lloyd-Jones at that time. It was at the Fountain Trust Conference in Guildford in 1971 that David, amongst many others, had his first encounter with Roman Catholics.

We invited David, together with about a dozen other speakers, to what turned out to be an important and historic occasion. As soon as it became known that Roman Catholics were being invited as speakers, we were strongly criticised by many. It had not been easy to persuade even the Council of the Fountain Trust to do such an adventurous thing. Some of my friends had reservations about the wisdom of what we agreed to do. I don't know what David felt. Anyway he did agree to come as a speaker. I think he was a little worried. David had not had much, if any, previous experience of meeting Roman Catholics, and certainly had not shared a platform with them. But the three Catholic speakers (Kevin Ranaghan, Roman Carter and George de Prizio) created an immensely wholesome impression for everyone at the Conference.

It was typical of David that he used such opportunities to talk personally with these men. He was concerned with the doctrinal differences that existed. But he came to the firm conclusion that these men were true Christians, who loved the Lord Jesus Christ and were honestly seeking to follow him as Lord. They were his brothers in Christ. It was also typical of David that once he had made up his mind about anything he would stick tenaciously to that opinion. There was no trace of doublemindedness in him.

The encounter at Guildford influenced David's future ministry in a number of important ways. Later on he was to be used by the Lord as an influence for good in Northern Ireland. One of the hunger strikers, Lane McClusky, came to know Christ through David's ministry and a Presbyterian minister, the Rev David Armstrong, was profoundly changed in his attitudes when he came into the sphere of David's influence. David Armstrong told viewers on television that David had changed his life. A Roman Catholic priest, Monsigneur Michael Buckley, said of David's ministry in Ireland, 'we have to pay a price for working for peace in Northern Ireland'. David walked side-by-side with Michael in a march for peace and had to face much anger from Evangelicals as a result.

David's conviction meant that many Roman Catholics took part in his missions and festivals of praise. David was never a 'party man'. Anglo-Catholics and Evangelical Anglicans alike welcomed his ministry and united in their support of his work. Yet the message was never adjusted to suit the audience. David always preached what he himself believed and presented it in a winsome and attractive manner.

However, in the early days of his ministry, according to his wife, Anne, David did not always have an open approach even to his fellow Anglicans. On television Anne shared how David's approach changed in their early years in York. 'David learned', she said, 'that fighting the establishment was not the way to go forward.'

As his outlook matured, so his influence spread wider. 'He was marvellously loyal to the institutional church', the former Archbishop of York said of him. Dr Stuart Blanch went on to describe the costliness of this witness. 'He was a burning and shining light', he said. 'But it was a costly business, for there is no cheap grace.' There was nothing cheap about David. He was not at all interested in projecting himself. He had no sleepless nights worrying about his self-image. He shared openly his pains as well as his pleasures, his weaknesses as well as his strong points.

David was one of the most fair-minded people I have ever known. He was transparently honest, a virtue which was particularly noticeable in the way he handled his final illness and whether or not God was going to heal him. He passed through controversial situations, but was never looking for trouble or wanting controversy for its own sake. He gave an important and impressive address at the National Evangelical Anglican Congress at Nottingham University in 1977. By this time he was becoming well known for his clear and precise teaching about Christian unity. In the course of his address he made a remark about the Reformation, and the divisions which resulted from it, which he regarded as unfortunate. A seemingly mild remark sparked off a number of personal attacks on him by those who regarded any criticism of the Reformation as almost blasphemy against the Holy Spirit. No doubt David's friendliness towards Roman Catholics, which by now had become well-known, triggered off this emotional response. A few strong-minded Evangelicals did refuse to co-operate with David's ministry, but they were a small minority; the majority recognised his integrity and the effectiveness of what he was doing. I believe that David's ministry helped forward proper ecumenism more than perhaps anyone else's in Britain during that time.

David Watson's view of the Church matured as the years passed. Brought up as a student in the evangelical world at Cambridge, and continuing to reflect that position in the first years of his ministry, it was only in later years that he developed an empathy for a more catholic view of the Church. This comes out in one of his best books, *I believe in the Church*. This book marked an important stage in his developing understanding of the Church as the Body of Christ, which, had he lived, would have made it possible for him to make even greater contributions to the understanding of the corporate people of God. It was his concern for the Church, and its unity in Christ, which was a most important check-balance to his main ministry and burden—that of evangelism. This influenced the way in which he planned with his team the various missions he held in cities, parishes and universities. My own bishop called David in to advise him on the relationship between his work and the churches. David explained the principles upon which he had developed his ministry over the years, the full extent of consultations which took place well beforehand, the invitations which had to be extended to him, the local leadership's approval, and the preparations which were carried through by the local leaders.

David tried to draw all Christians together for his missions, and usually succeeded in bringing together a wide cross-section of people. He worked tirelessly for Christian unity before, during and after the mission was over, for in the final analysis it was the preparation beforehand and the pastoral care afterwards which determined the success or otherwise of what happened. It is a tribute to his methods and to the sensitivity with which all these details were worked out, that his missions never divided churches; more unity was always one of the more obvious fruits of what he did. Unlike others, who only sought a few like-minded leaders to work with, David always strove for the widest possible support, and usually got it. The results that followed were therefore wholesome and unifying.

It was at an Evangelical Alliance conference at High Leigh, near London, in September 1982 that David gave a talk which was a clear explanation of his views on Christian unity. I was present and heard him. It was a courageous statement given in the face of some who were bound to disagree. He made abundantly clear his evangelical convictions, which had never wavered throughout the years. He shared the biblical principles upon which he built his work—certainly the most successful and fruitful evangelist of his generation in Britain. He then went on to spell out simply what he saw as the basis for Christian unity. It was being 'in Christ'. All those who were 'in Christ' were brothers and sisters and should treat each other as such.

We can all be very thankful that David Watson incorporated Christian reconciliation as an integral part of his message, linked closely with evangelism and renewal. This was obviously important in places like Northern Ireland where he ministered with such success. But his message also left an abiding impression elsewhere. He only visited Australia once, but I found several years later that his visit was still being talked about and particularly the theme of reconciliation which had fitted like a glove so many of the strained relationships in that country. Everywhere David went in Australia he was a focal point of unity, while at the same time preaching the gospel unequivocally with the winsomeness and skill which was the hallmark of his remarkable ministry. In the last few years of his life I was involved with David in several ventures to bring reconciliation between those working for renewal in the denominations and those who had split away and formed independent churches. His own church in York had been disturbed by this independent spirit, and a small group had left it, which caused deep hurt to David. Yet he was soon looking for reconciliation and peace in a very tense situation. He never spared himself in his quest for a united Christian witness.

David Watson was never a party man. Loyalty to the Lord and all his people was more important to him than support for a party in the Church. David discovered early on that 'party spirit' is a work of the flesh, not a gift of the Holy Spirit. David didn't wear sectarian blinkers and this meant that he was able to see more widely than many others. Prejudice was not part of his make-up. He always studied carefully and responsibly every new thing which came within sight. Some things he rejected; but once convinced of anything, he was fearless not only in preaching it, but also in living it himself whatever the personal cost. David became convinced early in his ministry of the social implications of the gospel; later he was happy to be identified closely with the new radical evangelicalism of men like Ron Sider, for whom he wrote the foreword to *Rich Christians in an Age of Hunger*. At the Anglican Renewal Conference in Canterbury in 1978 David was Chairman of the group that discussed evangelism. In their findings they stated 'we see in the gospel of the kingdom, God's concern with man's wholeness, in this life and beyond. Evangelism aims, therefore, for freedom and justice for the whole person. *We repudiate any dichotomy between evangelism and social action.* The principalities and powers are to be put to flight wherever they are entrenched against the cause of the kingdom. Christ judges and would renew not only people but the political and social structures in which they live and work.' This statement was the profound conviction that David held, and it was reflected in all his speaking and writing. He himself, together with Anne and their children, had a simple life-style. In York they opened their hearts and their home to others in a household community. David always wanted to allow every aspect of his life to reflect Christ and to exemplify his standards.

But for all that David would never have joined a social action party as such; it was just part of his life. Those aspects of David's life which may to others have seemed contradictory, were welded together in the fire of his own personal devotion to Christ and his unbounded love for people. Love was the determining influence of his life. What was true of his relationship to so-called 'social action' was also true of his link with the charismatic movement, which he influenced profoundly throughout his ministry.

Early in his ministry, particularly during his time at Cambridge as a curate, he became convinced of the need for Christians to be filled with the Holy Spirit and to exercise the spiritual gifts. He himself had such an experience and received the gift of tongues. David was clearly going to have a very influential ministry amongst Evangelicals. When the news got out about his experience he received many letters warning him of the dangers of pentecostalism. Extreme pressure was brought to bear upon him to renounce these excesses and have nothing to do with the emerging charismatic movement. But David was not to be deterred so easily. He had studied the Scriptures carefully. He had prayed earnestly about it. He had received this experience and it had blessed his life and ministry. Loyalty to his Lord was for him in this more important than anything else. From the moment he became convinced about this ministry of the Holy Spirit he began to teach and preach it, though with notable tact and grace; his whole approach was also so peaceable he never antagonised those with whom he disagreed. He never became a charismatic party man, and was for all his life a potent influence for reconciliation between Evangelicals on these issues. When John Stott and I agreed to hold a consultation for Anglican Evangelicals on these matters, David Watson was a member of the group and contributed much to the discussions and the ultimate publication of the report *Gospel and Spirit*, which helped so much to bring reconciliation and peace where before there had been so much bitterness and misunderstanding.

One of the sticking points with Evangelicals was the interpretation of the biblical phrase about being 'baptised in the Spirit'. Unlike many charismatics David believed that it was more correct to talk about being 'filled' with the Holy Spirit, and that the phrase 'baptism in the Spirit' was descriptive of regeneration and therefore referred to all Christians. He certainly believed in the need for a definite experience of being filled with the Spirit, but he was never dogmatic about this issue. If called upon he would graciously testify to what he had experienced. His eirenic approach made reconciliation between Evangelicals and charismatics much easier, and many Evangelicals were happy to involve David in ministry when they would not have invited people who professed more definite views and who expressed them in a 'take it or leave it' attitude.

When I was in Australia in September 1984 I was amazed to discover the depth of impact of David's visit in 1980 upon the churches. Everyone I spoke to talked to me about it, and several said they thought its benefits were increasing and had been greater after his death than before it. The same must be true of other places which David visited. Some of my Australian friends, who helped organise David's visit, had since that time read David's book *You Are My God*. In that book David describes in some detail the problems which his church in York was going through at the very moment he and his team were ministering in Australia. These problems caused David acute pain and anxiety, and there were a number of 'phone calls backwards and forwards between York and Australia. Some of my Australian friends knew about what was going on, though the majority didn't. All were amazed that David had been able to fulfil such a strenuous programme when he was bearing such personal strain. But perhaps this has a lot to do with the secret of David's power. He knew profoundly what it was to be 'dead in Christ' as well as full of resurrection life and power. He knew how to surrender earthly cares and leave them in the hands of his Lord. It would seem that far from diminishing David's effectiveness, the pain he was suffering was allowed to act redemptively. Paul was able to say 'when I am weak, I am strong' (2 Corinthians 12.10) and this was what David experienced in Australia. He simply gave the Holy Spirit even more room to move in. The account that many Australians have given me would confirm the truth of this.

Lord Tonypandy, the former Speaker of the House of Commons who knew David very well, said on television, 'If ever God spoke to our generation, he spoke through David Watson.' Many other leaders of Church and state would echo these words. Yet the more one got to know David the more one realised how costly it was for him to scale the heights of commitment and discipleship. His natural inclinations would have been to 'play safe' and to keep in the sheltered waters of a narrower and more strictly limited ministry. Instead he put to sea and was buffeted by the waves. Truly he launched into the deep and, like the disciples of Jesus before him, caught a large catch. He resolutely took the arduous pathway of love, which always risks rejection. As a result he suffered many wounds, which his sensitive nature must at times have found very hard to bear. His deep concern for Christian unity took him into many cross-fire situations, when it seems he got hit by both sides at once.

David would never have wanted to become a cult figure during his lifetime and certainly not after his death. Nevertheless we would be foolish not to learn lessons from such an outstanding Christian. What he lived and worked for must continue, and we need to remember the pattern he followed and the costly pathway to Christian unity which he took so faithfully. It is always the *person* who matters most, not the *views* that person may or may not hold. It was primarily because David was the person he was that the fruit accrued to God's glory. It would be a mistake simply to imitate his methods, sound though they were. David became the person he was because he allowed the Lord himself to shape his life. He clearly loved his Lord, and he loved everyone he met or came into contact with. It was this spirit which was so infectious and which others discovered; it is this spirit which we all need to have and to share with others.

Chapter Four

THE OUTREACH

by

Douglas Greenfield

Douglas Greenfield was for several years the administrator of the Belfrey Trust, with special responsibility for David Watson's missions and festivals.

I begin writing this commentary on certain aspects of the life and ministry of my dear friend David Watson amidst the towering, breathtaking mountains of the Austrian Alps. The scenery is unbelievably beautiful, the air rare and exhilarating, the terrain demanding and challenging. To attempt to climb these peaks one must pause to count the cost, and then come to terms with nature. In inclement weather, it is important to select the timing carefully before making a dash for the summit. There is a real sense in which David was always making a dash for the summit. Many of his fellow climbers found it difficult to keep pace with him: some gave up, settling for lower plateaus, others needed rest and attention part-way up, but many were stimulated to push higher into new experiences of God's love as he with them strove for the highest.

As Administrator for many years of David's outreach ministry, capsulated in city-wide missions, festivals of praise, seminars and local church Renewal Weeks, I was privileged to know and appreciate the 'man behind the message' both in a personal friendship and a working relationship. I question whether it could ever be said that one knew David fully, for his acute vulnerability caused him to develop a protective shell which was sometimes difficult to penetrate. I determine in this record to be wary of the unjustified or overuse of superlatives—it would be easy to fall into the trap, especially as on the occasions when the veil was drawn aside and the protection penetrated, one discovered a person of rare gifts, a gracious caring spirit, and deep spirituality. He was a man of faith, and this placed him in the risk-taking business. Always pushing back frontiers, he had a deep appreciation of God's ability to meet his need. As a former rugby player he fully understood and valued the comforting words from a team-mate 'with you' when the opposing pack was bearing down, and all that he needed to hear in his ventures of faith were God's words 'with you'.

David possessed a personal 'presence', embodying the virtues of athleticism—natural aptitude, intelligence, and sound habits formed through experience. He had courage and fortitude, virtues that must not be confused. Courage is the ability to face situations stamped by judgment as dangerous; fortitude is the ability to endure. The endurance may be extracted out of the experience rather than the anticipation of danger, and commonly it is reflected in the capacity to perform through pain. David was both a natural leader and a warm human being. Of all human attributes leadership is probably the hardest to define. It consists of the willingness to take decisions knowing that risk attaches to all choice. Effective leaders do not panic in the face of adversity, just as they are well-advised not to crow in moments of success. A good leader must also have the ability to effect the marriage between what needs to be done and what is possible. David had these God-given qualities of courage, judgment and modesty. He was a friend to all with whom he worked. It is a rare man who can control and direct, lead and umpire, and at the same time remain a friend.

St Cuthbert's church in York was the seedbed and launching pad for many of the developing ministries which David and his wife Anne had been pondering in their hearts for some time. Dance, drama, lively music, and extended families supporting full-time workers brought a whole new concept of a church in action. In order to accommodate the increasing numbers attending, St Michael-le-Belfrey, in the shadow of York Minster, was taken over at the eleventh hour before it was destined to become a museum for the Minster. A unique team from many backgrounds continued to gather around David and Anne and as the work further developed the activity was couched in a new understanding and experience of praise and worship. The beginnings of 'shared leadership' as opposed to 'delegation of authority' appeared. Strains and stresses were not unknown, pain and misunderstandings were frequently interwoven with the excitement and thrill of new things. The scriptural principle of 'a corn of wheat falling into the ground and dying' that new life might break forth was an ever-present experience for David and Anne at that time. They worked through the three stages encountered in the growth of any community—from honeymoon, through nightmare, to reality—and all this proved to be a necessary preparation for the next chapter.

David Watson was a great communicator, able to present the most profound matter in simple terms. He would have been a success in many walks of life and had he continued in the army or entered the Diplomatic Service his natural graciousness and integrity would have stood him in good stead. Occasionally on missions, either in the planning stages or during the actual events, we were faced with sticky situations making it necessary to deal with less than sympathetic officials. David hated confrontation and often spent sleepless nights after such occasions, always apologising in case of personal hurt to the other party. The time came when he felt the church ought to be sharing on a broader platform the things God was doing in St Michael's; he sensed a 'thermal of God's Spirit' and plunged into it. None of us could have imagined the far-reaching consequence of the brief 'phone call which he made to me late one night, asking if I would administer a Renewal Week.

Twelve Renewal Weeks were held between 1977 and 1982, when David and Anne left for London. Their attraction and credibility lay in the fact that they sought to be a reflection of the life of St Michael's. Theory was supported by experience. Guests living with congregation families for a week and sharing in the life of the church quickly saw the frailties and weaknesses, and yet it was through that very vulnerability that God spoke to so many—'when we are weak then he is strong'—'my strength is made perfect in weakness'. These weeks tapped a need, there was a ready response, and we had to limit the numbers wanting to come. One hundred and fifty visitors—the number we started off with—proved to be too many for our facilities and accommodation, and we levelled off at one hundred. The geographical pendulum swung frequently from Northern Ireland to Eire, Wales to Malta; there were representatives from Australia, New Zealand, South Africa, Canada, USA, Norway, Sweden, and many other countries, some behind the Iron Curtain. Support came from all the established denominations. In recent years other churches have caught the vision of holding similar weeks, and we have been able to encourage and guide them from our experience. We held seminars on small group leadership, spiritual gifts, and local church renewal. Drama, dance, music, counselling and shared leadership were undergirded by a spirit of praise and worship. On-going friendships were forged, with house and holiday exchanges. Programmes of team visits maintaining a vital link with represented churches formed part of the spin-off.

David saw that the world was our parish. Where would this vision end? It hasn't done so yet. The true test of a man's work for God is whether it continues after his death, and Renewal Weeks are still an important part of the life of St Michael's—two years after David's departure to London, and nine months after his death. The vision so far as God is concerned is inexhaustable, the need ever growing: 'I will build my church'. It is significant to note that the original vision of Renewal Weeks came through a word of prophecy. Obviously the church had been prepared by God for that word because it was received positively by the eldership... 'It seemed good to the Spirit and to us'. Many of the subsequent advances in David's ministry came this way, either through himself or Anne or through a member of the fellowship. Throughout the period of the Renewal Weeks when as a church we were giving out to others, we were ourselves in constant need of renewal and of greater spiritual maturity. It was dangerous to rely on past blessings. One Swiss pastor, having returned home from a Renewal Week, wrote:

> We had heard that St Michael-le-Belfrey was an almost perfect church. We could hardly believe it, but we praised the Lord. Now we have been to York personally, now we have seen. It is not perfect and now we praise the Lord even more. If the Lord can use sinners such as the people in St Michael's, he can use us too.

Many of the participants in our Renewal Weeks were leaders in their own churches, and David proved to have a particular gift in communicating the principles of church growth, drawing upon his wide experience in bringing two virtually redundant churches to life. The joys and sorrows, frustrations and hopes set some of those ministers and pastors aflame as they reviewed their own ministries from a distance. Those parishes from whence they came felt the impact of their renewed vision and changed lives. Reports are still coming in of whole parishes going on from strength to strength after Renewal Week visits and there was undoubtedly a momentum of the Spirit confirming that the original vision was correct. David recognised the importance of spelling out the theological basis behind renewal. Many guests came with all sorts of preconceived ideas about St Michael's, but as the week unfolded and we all relaxed on the Saturday evening with an entertainment which included mime and drama, the more nervous guests settled down—realising they had not come into a wild spiritual hothouse. People were hungry to receive more of God and his Spirit, and many were the testimonies of blessing received. One guest remarked—'Here we felt God's love in action. We go back believing he goes with us'.

David was never a triumphalist, he never maintained that unless all is going well, and is seen to be going well, then we have let God down. Instead his position was—'though the fig trees have no fruit, and no grapes grow on the vines, though the olive crop fails, and the fields produce no corn, even though the sheep all die and the cattle stalls are empty...I will still be joyful and glad because the Lord God is my Saviour...' He frequently challenged us with the words—'Where does our security lie? How far can we go on trusting God when we have no experience of his love? He often knew that condition, and those who were closest to him learned to agonise as well as praise with him.

71

Many new things were launched by David at this stage in his ministry. He held firmly to the view that the Spirit of God is the Spirit of movement, and it is important to discern when spiritual momentum begins to wane. So often we want to hold on, keep a thing going, have this or that meeting because we have always had it, prop it up at all costs, when we should be realising that the Spirit of God has withdrawn himself in order to do a new thing. If we stay in one place too long we run the risk of becoming stale and stagnant. David would teach—'He who has an ear, let him hear what the Spirit is saying to the churches. Traditionalism can be a great hindrance to a work of the Spirit. The aim and vision of Renewal Weeks can be summed up in the cry of the psalmist—'Wilt thou not revive us again, that thy people may rejoice in thee' (Psalm 85.6).

Although David was a most effective pulpit preacher and had built up a national reputation as such, he worked most effectively when in harness with a team. Way back in 1973 he had been encouraged by various Christian leaders to consider leading city-wide missions. This would be a departure from leading the university missions with which he had been involved for many years. Looking back, the concept must have seemed somewhat foreign to him. Shy by nature, a retiring personality, planning, business and finance not his strong points, he was certainly a man not given to the powerful evangelistic thrust of Billy Graham. Could he ever be effective in a Harringay or Wembley setting? In keeping with the 'small is beautiful' era of the early seventies, he liked home evangelistic evenings where an on-going contact could be maintained with those attending. And yet when one or two invitations came to lead city-wide missions in 1974-5, he began to re-think. The next plan of God for David was being revealed. 'Not my ability Lord, but my availability is what matters. Here am I, Lord, send me'.

In Sheffield a total of 13,000 people attended the mission, and four hundred gave their lives to Christ. Quickly the name 'mission' was changed to 'festival' because the preaching of the gospel was undergirded by celebration, praise and worship. Here was a new combination in large gatherings, presenting the claims of the cross, but with a celebration which scattered the gloom and depression of the national scene. David began to experience a third way in which God wanted to work. He had already seen God at work in the cell (the small house groups) and in the congregation (at St Cuthbert's, St Michael's and many a church congregation around the country).

Now it was time for the celebration, where people come together in great numbers from a wide area across the denominational board; members of one family all seeking to proclaim the good news of Jesus Christ and to encourage each other in the faith. He was supported in this new-look ministry by various groups who sang and led in worship, but always in the back of his mind was the thought that sooner or later he must form his own team, trained into the same vision, able to travel for set periods of time, but ideally with a resource centre to return to after the festivals were over. Where better to look for such a team than in the church where it had not only all begun, but where it was still going on, his own spiritual home—St Michael's. Music, dance and drama combined to enhance that triple springboard of ministry—evangelism, spiritual renewal and reconcilation—from which he now was launched on to the world scene.

This new phase of ministry, which got under way in 1977 with a major commitment in Northern Ireland, was to continue, naturally with variations in team members, almost until the day he died. One of the saddest moments of my life was when I sat with him shortly before he went to be with his Lord, and we decided that he would not be able to make the visit to Sweden which we had planned together.

We realised that because of the size and scope of these developing festivals, they must be researched and planned carefully. We approached them like a task-force reconnoitring a strategic territory. When an invitation came, I carried out a study of the history of missions over past years in the area. We looked at the social and political background: unemployment, denominational breakdown, church attendance figures, population, and the balance between rural and urban areas. With each festival, we aimed to reach an area stretching for twenty-five miles around the given centre. David studied it all, trimming his message, gearing his approach, getting the right emphasis, delicately balancing humour with 'straight from the shoulder' preaching. At one period we were turning down around seventy percent of all invitations—for many reasons. Occasionally we felt the area was not ready for an outreach of this kind; sometimes we sensed we were not the right people for the task. When, in conjunction with those issuing the initial invitation, we felt it right to respond positively, committees came into being and the long process of preparation began.

Ideally we spent eighteen months to two years in preparation. I have worked in many parts of the world with many people both in secular and spiritual capacities, but I have never been stimulated, challenged or stretched more than during those years I was privileged to share in outreach and evangelism with David Watson. Because my role was 'going before' preparing the way, he would sometimes introduce me as John the Baptist, to which I would respond—'I do not mind the term, always providing I have a better end!'

Those who have worked closely with others on teams, especially in a travelling situation, will readily understand the pressures and tensions which can easily arise. David, like the rest of the team, frequently proved to have 'feet of clay'. During the long absences from home he would wonder how Anne and the children were faring, whether St Michael's was holding together, when he would be struck by an attack of asthma. Meanwhile he would be battling with the satanic pressures and doubts with which all those who dare to fly in the face of the enemy must contend. The other side of the coin, however, was 'all joy'. Great bonds which can never be broken were forged within the team.

There were also some hilarious moments. One of our team members records a vivid memory of David when they were all at Toronto airport, following a fairly intense mission. 'We were all tired, but relaxed and David reached over to one of our bags which contained a long peroxide blond wig (one of our props!) which he then proceeded to try on. Having decided that he would pass as a rock star in it, he began to act the part, beating out a rhythm on an imaginary guitar, giggling as he did so. Needless to say, the team were delighted by this spontaneous outburst, despite the amazement of our fellow travellers!'

With the increasing demand for festivals, the administration and organisation had to grow accordingly. We had at first relied upon local committees to provide their own public address systems, with all the accompanying weaknesses as they tried to grapple with church pillars, balconies, and buildings which acoustically were never meant to cope with modern day music. Eventually we purchased a trailer and towed our own PA system around the country; latterly we employed a professional Christian company which lifted the whole responsibility away from us, and we were indeed grateful! Prior to the professionals taking over, the bonds of Christian charity in the team were often stretched to breaking-point as the mixer broke down, flexes were found to be too short, and plugs the wrong type, whilst David (who was not the world's greatest practical technician) looked on tensely. Many a quick prayer-meeting was held just before taking the stage at the start of a festival evening, for the express purpose of restoring some equanimity to a distraught PA team!

Getting the timing right for a festival was crucial. Sometimes the Christian church embarks too easily upon 'mission' with motives less than the highest. In an initial planning meeting with leaders who had invited us to consider a festival I asked the question 'Why do you want a mission?' One gentleman stood up and said, 'Well, we haven't had one in this area since John Wesley, and we feel we ought to be doing something!' This was commendable, but was it a sufficient reason to embark upon an outreach of this nature? Three criteria were applied in seeking God's timing. These were put to local leaders in the first planning meeting in the form of three questions:

1. Is there a holy discontent with things spiritual in the area?
2. Is there any evidence, however small, that God has already begun to do a new thing?
3. Are there those who are willing to pay the price for spiritual renewal?

Faithful answers to these questions were of considerable help, both to local leaders and to ourselves, enabling us to get a 'line of faith' as to what God wanted to do. If replies were positive, then together we would 'speak the word of faith'.

Off the platform, David was retiring by nature; on the platform he was vibrant, authoritative and totally sincere. Like Wesley, a knight of the burning heart. Occasionally a law unto himself, but always prepared to listen to others and work under authority. In York this meant working with the elders of St Michael's church, and later in London with the trustees of the Belfrey Trust. He was meticulous in the preparation of his messages and unceasing in the work-load he undertook. In retrospect I believe he knew there were not many years left; why else should he, at the comparatively young age of 49, feel any urgency to write his autobiography—against the advice of many?

Disciplined with himself and expecting that same discipline from those with whom he worked, he would co-operate with all those who truly belonged to Christ. He would say: *'If any man be in Christ he is a new creation.* Therefore, irrespective of his denomination or churchmanship, he is my brother; if Christ has received him, so must I.' His ministry was acceptable across our nation and other nations. People felt they could trust him. Here was a man willing to be vulnerable, wearing his heart on his sleeve, credible because he spoke from personal experience. His was a rich understanding of the breadth of God's kingdom.

In all our festivals David was committed to the healing of broken relationships amongst God's people. He was broken-hearted at the fragmentation that had taken place in Christendom, often because of personality cults or an unwillingness to come under discipline and authority. His personal suffering bore testimony to the fact that 'grace is never cheap'. He frequently passed through the 'dark night of the soul'. Particularly on missions he was occasionally plunged into what can only be described as Gethsemane experiences—'My God, why has thou forsaken me?'

His depressions were sometimes fearful to behold, and at such times no one could really reach him. These would rub off on to the team, and the fact that they worked through such times, were not destroyed, and kept the ministry going, speaks highly of their spiritual quality both as individuals and as a team. The Lord always undertook for these occasions, but little did observers know the agony we were sometimes passing through on our tours. We found through experience that one or two months away from the home situation was too long for David. Concern for the family back home and the uncertainty of asthma attacks, revealed that a maximum of two to three weeks on tour was all both he and the team could reasonably handle.

He loved to introduce people to Christ, for he himself had fallen in love with Jesus Christ and knew that on-going anointing of his Spirit. His lovely description of the anointing of the Spirit was that of the Lord 'coming toward us to kiss'. 'Love and trust people unconditionally as Jesus did' he would say 'You may get disillusioned or even hurt in the process, but this drives away fears and melts down barriers. Don't ask the question *why*, but rather *what*. *What* do you want my attitude to be; *what* are you saying to me?'

This recollection by one of our team gives a moving insight into David's heart—

Our last mission with him was spent in Ireland, beginning in Belfast and ending in Dublin. It was a place which held special memories for him due to his awareness of the spiritual hunger and openness of the many Christians he had met there, from both sides of the border. The team used to pray with David before each festival and on this occasion, we prayed specifically for his asthma, as he was concerned that it might prevent him from speaking clearly. His back was also very painful, for the cancer had started to make it difficult for him to stand for any length of time. Added to this, he had a mouth infection which had developed as a reaction to the drugs he was taking for the asthma. The day was cold and grey and one of the dancers was feeling particularly miserable at the prospect of having to remain bare-footed during the worship time. (One frequently danced with no feeling in one's feet!) After our prayer time the dancer disappeared to the dressing-room reserved for the women on the team. As I made my way to the same room David, rather breathless, asked me where she had gone. I arrived, seconds later, to see David kneeling down vigorously rubbing her feet to warm them. After he had massaged them for about six minutes he stopped and, between wheezes and coughs, told us laughingly that we'd better pray that he would be able to make it to the stage. The three of us prayed together, with David holding one of us on either side. After we had finished praying, David remained motionless for several seconds, as if trying to savour the moment. Both the dancer and I were silent after David had left the room, as we both realised how much of a physical sacrifice it had been to David, as well as a real display of Christ-like humility.

In 1979 there was a strong possibility of a festival being held in Malta at the invitation of Roman Catholic friends, both priests and lay folk, many of whom had visited York for Renewal Weeks. I visited the island and researched the situation in depth with positive reactions. All seemed set and David and I made a preliminary visit, speaking at various small meetings in preparation for an eight-day tour. Having personally visited Malta over many years I enthused him with the thought of the sunshine.

We arrived in a hurricane, torrential rain and three inches of water on the runway. Our first meeting with leaders was within an hour of landing and we sat through it in very wet clothes. However the warmth of fellowship was something he never forgot, and it was one of the great sadnesses of those touring years for David that due to last minute objections—not from Roman Catholics, but from the Chancellor of the Anglican Cathedral in Valetta—the visit was never fulfilled. We were hoping to make plans together for a possible visit in 1985, but that was not to be.

In a few short years David helped change the face of religious life in his own and many other countries. Due to the power of the mass media and with a ministry not confined to any one denomination or emphasis of thought, he was probably the most prayed for man. One leader in Australia where very significant festivals were held in Sydney, Brisbane, Melbourne, Adelaide and other centres, summed up David's appeal to all shades of religious persuasion by remarking 'He is unclassifiable'.

After the last Swedish mission toward the end of 1983, which we conducted without him because he was too ill to travel, a Swedish pastor bidding me farewell at the airport remarked 'David is not indispensable, but he is irreplaceable'.

'A light has gone out' proclaimed the front page of a national newspaper the morning after David's death. His memorial lies in the changed lives of untold numbers of folk around the world who by the power of Christ working through David's ministry have been transformed—in the number of churches and fellowships now enjoying something of that power that made the early church so vibrant with spiritual expectation.

His cry 'The Lord reigns' closed so many of our festivals. That cry must go on and will go on, if Christendom continues to take heed of what he experienced and taught. Perhaps the supreme thing about David was that he was willing to 'dare for God'.

Chapter Five

RIDING LIGHTS

by

Paul Burbridge

Paul Burbridge is the Artistic Director of the Riding Lights Theatre Company and the co-author with Murray Watts of *Lightning Sketches* and *Time to Act*.

Looking back on several years of close involvement with David Watson's public ministry, I wonder how many of those who invited us to lead missions and festivals noticed a certain incongruity in what was going on, and found this funny or even slightly alarming? Everyone was keen to talk to the constantly immaculate, blue-blazered, well-combed figure of David Watson, but when he introduced the members of his team there would be a brief moment of silence. Not that they were expecting football team jerseys but they might well have anticipated a group of eager young clergymen, or smiling people with big Bibles and 'I AM A COUNSELLOR' badges, even ladies with handbags and large brooches. Instead, our welcoming committees had to stifle their surprise and shake hands with or say a rather self-conscious 'Hi!' to a bunch of somewhat disreputable-looking actors, musicians and dancers. (Maybe it was only the male actors who were disreputable-looking?)

What did others make of David plus a group of beards, leg-warmers, jeans, shawls, bomber-jackets, duffel coats and men in knee-length boots? What did David make of it? I wonder if he ever inwardly flinched as he introduced us? If he did, he never showed it. He always taught us that our preaching should be answering questions raised by our lifestyle, but should we have been raising eyebrows in response to our hairstyle? Anyway there we were, David and the team. We never found a name, so remained the team by default, though the more cynical observer might have seen us as 'the travelling circus'. Posters would go up outside city halls advertising 'David Watson and his team from York'. How many of the average passers-by started having thoughts about bears or even huskies? In reality we were David Watson's friends and Christian brothers and sisters; that was the way he treated and cared for all those who worked alongside him. It was one of the greatest privileges of my life to have been 'on the team'.

Corporate communication was the driving force behind working with a group; together we could demonstrate the renewal of the Body of Christ in a small way, which, on his own, the big-name evangelist can never do. David shunned the personality cult. The question remains as to why David was so keen to develop drama within his ministry at all, especially as the drama which developed was of a particular brand. Various adjectives have often been used to describe the sketches which we performed: 'humorous', 'zany', 'punchy', 'hard-hitting'. Here again, some might have found a note of incongruity; others might have found these same sketches 'irreverent' or even the whole idea of dramatising the gospel message offensive. If they did, few concessions were made to them. There were no flowing robes, solemn faces or sonorous voices; none of the wooden banalities of traditional religious drama. The style was a Christian mixture of the Bible, the *Beano* and *Beyond The Fringe*. How did all this fit in with David's straightforward, clear, unemotional style of evangelism? Where did it come from?

I met David in February 1973 in Oxford, where I was in my first year, studying English Literature. David had come to lead the Christian Union's mission to the university. He had already been using occasional sketches and dramatic readings provided by York students and other members of the congregation at St Cuthbert's, mainly for guest services both in the church and in the Minster. He had come to Oxford with a couple of these in his briefcase, hoping to find someone to perform them. The President of the Christian Union was a member of my college, so I got the job. In fact, I also got *The Job*, which is the one monologue I particularly remember having to learn. The only line that remains with me now is (shouting), 'I curse the day on which I was born!' From the warmth of the response in the Union Debating Chamber, this must have struck a chord with my colleagues at the University! Whatever else it might *not* have been in terms of a watershed for Christian theatre, it was the beginning of a chain of events which took me two years later to York, where I was welcomed into David and Anne's household. This, after a further two years, led to the establishment of a professional theatre company in York under the name of Riding Lights. Initially, I had been invited as a voluntary church worker to develop drama at St Michael-le-Belfrey and in connection with the widespread evangelistic and renewal ministry which was steadily rippling out beyond the local church as each invitation dropped into our little pool. Acting and the theatre had been major interests for me throughout school and university, so David's invitation to York seemed to provide a good opportunity to continue to explore the relationship between my Christian faith and any long-term professional involvement with the theatre.

Many people at St Michael's, including David, gave

me great encouragement in this exploration, even though
it meant sets being built in his kitchen and the garage
being usurped by a brightly-painted governess's cart,
which had become a *sine qua non* of our early street
theatre. The local drama group at St Michael's grew
quickly and produced some good work for the various
services. We tried to produce something every two weeks
or so. Away from home, on the missions, resources
shrank and I was stretched. I soon exhausted my stock of
one-man material but there was at least one other person
who could help out with the sketches—David. He drew
the line at parts which called for bowler hats and red
noses but said he was happy to be 'a narrator or something'. Our stage debut was a piece about Jonah for the
Christian Union at Durham university, who were preparing for a forthcoming mission. David played narrator,
God and the whale. (I took him at his word!)

Few preachers have matched David's voice for richness
of tone and ease of listening. I'm sure that many who
have heard him would agree. Few people also know
that, like an actor, he spent a lot of time in his early
preaching days having regular voice lessons from a professional actress. In private conversation, David would
often talk at great speed which sometimes led to amusing
vowel abbreviations. As far as I recall, he led missions in
'Manch'ter', 'Liv'pool' and 'Bor'muth' and regularly
worked with a theatre company called 'Rine Lights',
who were, 'very pahful salways'. It is a brave man who
surrounds himself with actors, who tend to fall without
mercy on any idiosyncrasies of speech and expression. I
often find myself chuckling affectionately when I
remember David, laughing as he recognised himself
parodied on the rostrum or just giggling helplessly with
us in the back of the Land-rover as we trundled home
after a mission meeting. For David, laughter was a God-

given antidote to his own depression and to many of the tensions which enveloped us in the daily spiritual battle. Sometimes this laughter worried me since with his severe asthma, David was often fighting for breath. The funnier things were, the more dangerous it looked.

Laughter—the kind that can give a wonderful sense of relief and well-being—was an important ingredient in the message we proclaimed; it was part of the joy of the Lord which we wanted to share with others. On a less spiritual level, too, the laughter occasioned by some of the sketches helped to lighten the intense atmosphere that is often characteristic of big evangelistic events. The response as people relaxed and mentally undid their top buttons was not unlike releasing a pressure cooker: hundreds of Christians, clasping their songsheets with moist palms, hoping for conversions, glancing across at their equally nervous non-Christian friends, who would be trying not to get noticeably involved, either with the songsheets or with what was going on on stage...for instance a sketch about the apostle Peter's miraculous escape from prison in the book of Acts:

Narrator One:	Soon Peter arrived outside the house where his friends were praying.
Narrator Two:	He knocked loudly. (*Peter knocks loudly offstage*)
One:	(*deep in prayer*) O Lord, we do just continue to pray, Father...
Two:	That you will come to our brother Peter in his cell...
One:	Encouraging him...
Two:	Supporting him...
One:	Assuring him that he has not been forgotten. (*Knocking*)

Two: And let us not be distracted, Lord.
         (*Knocking*)
One: Lord, as you look down on Peter now...
Two: We pray, Father, that you will hear his cry.
Peter: (*Off*) 'Open up!'
One: And, Lord, whoever that is...
Two: Will you calm him...
One: And give him your peace.
Peter: 'LET ME IN!'

Extract from *In the Nick of Time*, Lightning Sketches (Hodder and Stoughton)

The fact that we could find humour under the surface of the biblical narratives and even laugh at ourselves went a long way to establishing a rapport with the audience on which David could then build. I'm glad that there was a group of us with him to share the funny moments on the missions but more importantly to help to shoulder a burden which would have otherwise been immensely heavy for one man to carry. I remember Anne saying that she breathed secret sighs of relief when she saw David going off on a mission with some friends in the passenger seats.

Another significant strand that was woven into the pattern, as David's use of drama developed, can be traced back to the work I was doing with Murray Watts during vacations from our respective universities. Murray was a lifelong friend and even as children we had dreamt about starting a theatre company of our own. For a short period each summer we ran an evangelistic street theatre project in North Wales with friends from university. The group was called Breadrock. It seemed like a good name at the time. It started as a 'drama-in-the-village-hall' project but after several days we soon discovered what was going on: everyone was down at the pub of an evening, not in the village hall at all. So we took our sketches and our songs to the pub car park and persuaded people to come outside for half an hour, with the promise of a cup of coffee and a chat afterwards if they liked the show. A surprising number did. Many of the modern versions of parables and the scriptural mimes which later achieved a kind of classic status under David's ministry were premièred in that car park. So were the false-bearded prophets, the music hall narrators, the bowler-hatted wisemen and the red-nosed fools, for that matter. Street theatre generated a style which demanded immediacy, colour, energy, zany humour and a kind of 'grab them before they drift off again' entertainment, coupled with a longing to communicate our faith in Jesus Christ to people who would never normally go near a church. We made ourselves as clear and as simple and as entertaining about the gospel as we possibly could. Perhaps this is why we got on so well with David? We found that we could switch from moments of hilarity to those of great stillness and seriousness without a sense of contradiction; both could be performed with integrity.

David responded unhesitatingly to the excitement of street theatre and the possibilities of this in York on the forecourt of St Michael's. His enthusiasm for this kind of lively contact with people never waned and years later he would have us out on the streets in freezing weather, drawing crowds and performing sketches while he, warmly clad in a polar jacket, gave brief 'links' to the programme. He thrived on it: so did we—in the summer!

With theatre of this kind we were able to 'preach' with David in many unorthodox contexts, where communication would have been almost impossible without the theatrical element. Wensleydale cheese factory seems to stand out in the memory for some reason but also many shopping centres, college bars, factory canteens, prisons and even the office of an insurance company, once the desks and filing cabinets had been pushed to the side.

Emboldened by the anonymity of the open air, members of our audience often felt quite free to join in our performances, either to heckle David or to make unfunny additions to the sketches. Did they feel this was the best way to audition for the team? We pressed on regardless, if humanly possible. Occasionally we failed to tone down the exuberance and the circus mentality of our street theatre sketches when performing inside church buildings. This produced conflicting reactions within the congregation, which a little more decorum might have prevented; as with any fair-ground, there were swings and round-abouts. A sketch performed by Breadrock at an evening guest service in St Michael's, based on the parable of the great banquet, went into considerable detail establishing the extent of the preparations for the party to which people were then going to refuse to come; effete choreographers, French chefs, men blowing up balloons and rushing in and out of the wine cellar, court jesters and despairing butlers pursued each other round the stage in a glorious blur of anticipated festivity. According to some the Holy Spirit was grieved; on the other hand there were at least two members of the public, amazed by what they saw through the open doors of the church, who came in, sat down agog and gave their lives to Christ at the end of David's sermon.

When the demand for these biblical sketches grew to the point where they were successfully published in a book called *Time to Act*, David wrote in the foreword 'I have consistently witnessed their extraordinary effectiveness in communicating the good news of Jesus Christ.' He wasn't just being kind: by the grace of God we *had* seen that happening. Contrary to the misgivings of many people, God was beginning to use drama in a remarkable way. As in so many areas of spiritual growth, David had been ahead of the tide in encouraging new methods and sensing where the Spirit of God was leading his church. 'God is a God of drama,' he wrote. 'Nothing could be greater "drama" than the incarnation itself, when God became flesh in Jesus Christ. Here is God's supreme communication of himself and yet the Church has too often dulled this by a profusion of spoken words.' For a man who used the spoken word so cogently and so articulately, this was a typically gracious acknowledgment of the complementary gifts of others. In time, the binding together of the spoken word and the visual illustration on the public platform became so natural that, in Eric Morecambe's immortal phrase to explain his colleague's alleged toupé, 'You could hardly see the join.' During our last major university mission together (Oxford 1982), David was using three sketches each night, weaving them into his talk to make one complete statement of a gospel theme. Argument, illustration, laughter, applause, exposition and challenge flowed without a break. Many students responded to that challenge.

David's ability to construct a talk was outstanding and full of his own sense of the dramatic. He sometimes described constructing a talk in terms of building a house —the illustrations were the windows. When he paused for a sketch, however, it was more like pausing for a plate-glass patio door. He strove for clarity and for simplicity without ever being naive and he spoke with an authority that was never overbearing. It was the authority of God. As writers of sketches we learnt a great deal from David's unerring gift of cutting out the waffle. He also developed another strategic gift: the brilliant knack of always making our sketches *appear* highly relevant to his theme, even though by the end of a ten-day festival we didn't always have a new sketch that was completely on target. But then he interpreted his own themes very widely. A favourite theme of the Holy Spirit, for instance, (always a hard one to dramatise, but impossible to avoid with an evangelist like David) would be explained in very practical terms, so a sketch dealing with gossip or our disinclination to get involved with other people's lives and problems would become a potent illustration of the need for the Holy Spirit in our hearts.

As we became more organised, a familiar pattern of useful evangelistic and renewal themes emerged, so we deliberately wrote material which we knew would fit well with what David would be preaching: sketches about forgiveness, commitment to one another, worship, death and resurrection, the Second Coming, the Cross, sketches for youth nights, warm-up sketches and some which might make use of the dancers on the team from time to time. We held daily meetings to pray and discuss what we felt God was saying. These often ended up with us revising plans laid three weeks before; we went off to write a new sketch and David went off to write a new talk. In this way the communication stayed fresh and prophetic—what God was saying *today*, to *this* group of people, in *this* university/city/church. It was exciting working under that kind of creative pressure but it also required great trust. Developing this trust in open and loving relationships was the key to the whole work. At no time did we feel that we appeared with David on big civic stages such as the Free Trade Hall or the Albert Hall, merely as professional performers doing a job. Our art was subservient to and flowing from the work of the Holy Spirit among us. At least, we prayed that that might be true.

Nonetheless we were professionals; supported by our church at home, earning our three pounds a week pocket-money and devoting our time and skills solely to the work in hand. 'So what do you chaps do for a living? I mean what do you do during the day when you aren't, um, doing what you're doing?' If I could have had five pence for the number of times Christians asked me that, I could have handed back the three pounds a week! To be fair, it was an unusual situation, not just because a group of actors were helping with the evangelism, but more significantly because families and households in a local church were supporting the actors. The Church of the Middle Ages had a strong tradition of patronage of the arts, though latterly the connection has hardly been so evident. As our roots were in York, comparisons were sometimes made between our sketches and the old Medieval Mystery Play Cycles, but how many people realised that the real resemblance was not so much in the parallels between ancient and modern biblical dramatisations but that the church was again giving tangible encouragement to its artists? Support wasn't coming officially from the Church but sacrificially from individual Christians in a local church which was beginning to understand the vital importance of the arts in society and the need for Christian artists to be freed to try to influence the surrounding culture through their work. The church became our Arts Council. An interesting and fruitful concept, but unfortunately there are few other churches working in this way. How different our culture might be in ten years time if more were to join them!

In the early days of drama being used in York, David must have sensed the need for a more professional standard on certain big occasions such as guest services in York Minster, to which up to two thousand people might come. In 1973 he invited Richard Everett, for many years artistic director of the Upstream Theatre Club in Waterloo, to bring a group of professional Christian actors from London to contribute some sketches to just such an occasion in the Minster. Time has washed away, even from Richard's mind, most of the memories of exactly what was performed, but he vaguely remembers two pieces; one on the Creation, 'with a group of actors pretending to be mud,' and another sketch which involved 'putting silver boxes over our heads in an attempt to shut out the voice of God.' These were early days. The situation served to highlight another important issue, however; David was apparently unprepared for the fact that the group had incurred travelling expenses of about a hundred pounds coming up from London on the train. As he gritted his teeth and paid the bill, I'm sure that he was wishing he could have called on professional help more locally. His own ministry was expanding rapidly and vast numbers were turning up. Obviously, if the other ingredients in the presentation apart from his preaching were to be able to sustain this kind of exposure, professional expertise was going to be needed regularly and would have to be integrated into the life of the local church. In music and dance there were already several people in the congregation who could more than rise to the situation. Most of us came from elsewhere to act though within a few months we forgot that we had done so. York became home.

His professional attitude to our work was comparable with the high standards David set himself in preparing his sermons. He was certainly not like one minister I heard of who, while he enjoyed the talents of the musicians in his congregation, always encouraged them to make a few mistakes to keep them humble. One wonders whether he applied the same principles to his own job—dropping the baby in the font or marrying the bride and the best man—just to keep himself humble? While each of us on the team could bring professionalism to bear on our own specialist skill, we also had to learn how to minister to people in a variety of other ways:

leading in prayer, leading in worship, singing, playing instruments, giving short talks and counselling were skills which all of us tried to cultivate if possible.

Despite the earliest English stage tradition which had its roots firmly within the liturgy of the Church, the use of theatre to proclaim the Christian message in 1975 was still felt to be something of a novelty and, for some, a dangerous one, since it ran such a great risk of contamination with 'the world'. For a few hundred years certain pietistic Christian groups, including many Evangelicals, had refused to have anything to do with the theatre. The theatres were often such hotbeds of vice and corruption as to justify this reaction in general; several theatres were closed down completely after Christian protest in the seventeenth century. Somehow this historical problem was perpetuated as a modern taboo—Christians, or at least many of the evangelical Christians I knew, were suspicious of theatre and its associations. It is not difficult to understand how a taboo is inherited and why the theatre continued to give itself a bad name in many cases but it is harder to understand how a faith that is based on redemption must declare certain important areas of human endeavour to be beyond the redemptive work of God. Sadly, several gifted actors and actresses of my parents' generation were firmly persuaded to give up the theatre when they were converted and advised to do something more constructive with their time, like teaching or nursing. Some felt torn apart in the process. What they needed and what the Church needed were Christian leaders to champion the cause of the Christian performer; to explain from the Bible that God is the God of the *whole* of life and communicates 'in many and various ways' (Hebrews 1.1); to make room for their gifts within the Church and to stir them up to challenge the values of a godless society. At St Michael's there was a growing understanding and appreciation of the arts as a natural enrichment of our lives, our worship and our outreach. The climate of Christian thinking has thankfully been changing in recent years not least due to David's very positive attitude towards the arts. As Riding Lights Theatre Company, we have always faced our critics, defended our work and received letters of complaint now and again but, like David, we entered the debate from a practical point of view; we tried to *show* people what we meant, rather than hold perhaps fruitless discussions. Initially, under the broad umbrella of David's ministry it was possible to do this quite rapidly. Thousands of Christians saw us in a short space of time. Perhaps some of the confidence now placed in Riding Lights was originally confidence in David and a preparedness to give the things he believed in at least a chance to prove themselves.

I had joined the Watson household in October 1975. The first major mission happened in November in Sheffield. The Fisherfolk were coming to look after the music. I was panicking at the thought of having to look after the drama alone so I invited the only member of Breadrock whom I knew was free to come with us. A few months later I found him sharing my room at the Rectory on a permanent basis and keeping me up late with his mime exercises. Geoffrey Stevenson is one of those multi-talented people who could have been a theologian, an actor, a mime or a chef. After a couple of years as a Riding Lights actor and a year or two as a chef in The Mustard Seed, he settled for mime and is now well-known in that capacity, relegating all the other activities to his spare time.

I knew that I had reached a certain level of trust in my relationship with David when he allowed me to assist him in leading a short mission at his old school. Wellington College. I remembered to take the bowler hat and the red nose for the sketches in chapel; I packed the scripts to be hastily rehearsed with whoever I could press-gang into taking part; the main problem was remembering the jacket and tie. The other thing indelibly imprinted in my brain was the awesome silence in the chapel, which became more profound each time I performed a sketch or David told one of his jokes. Things loosened up on day two but I could well imagine some of the derogatory comments made in the Senior Common Room.

While I was thus engaged that year (1975-6), Murray Watts was in Hoylake writing plays in his attic. Eventually the experience got to him and while absorbed with an angels' scene in his play *The Tree that Woke Up*, he came downstairs and made two cups of tea—one for himself and one for the angel. So his doctor told me! Back in York, people would say to me, 'Oh, you must meet Nigel Forde, he's an ACTOR.' I'm not sure what that made me but the implication was clear: there was another professional actor lurking somewhere around the congregation at St Michael's. Nigel was a difficult person to meet as his work took him away from home between Monday and Saturday. I discovered that he was also a writer and had been working in the theatre in the northeast for ten years, including a spell at York Theatre Royal. He and his wife Hilary had recently become Christians through St Michael's. I discussed with Nigel the idea, which Murray and I had already considered, of starting a professional theatre company of Christian actors based in York, closely linked with the work at the church. He said that he'd tried running a company in York before and it hadn't worked. It couldn't be done. So we did it! A year later Nigel, Murray and myself set about starting Riding Lights, and Nigel's experience of running unsuccessful theatre companies in York was to prove invaluable!

Preparations for the start of Riding Lights were actually made more from Nottingham than from York. In October 1976, I had left the Watsons temporarily to spend a year at St John's College in Nottingham doing a post-graduate diploma in Theology. David and I discussed this idea while walking on the hills above the cottage which the family used to visit near Helmsley. I was keen to take up the opportunity of some further academic training to undergird the dramatisations of biblical material which we were producing. Visual images tend to linger in the mind and we wanted to try and avoid leaving false impressions. Missions were still going ahead so Murray (who had also come to St John's for a year) and I were released from our courses to accompany David and the team to Leeds and on the first of a series of visits to Belfast.

A great incentive to the cause of setting up a professional company was given from an unexpected quarter that year. In April 1977, the National Evangelical Anglican Congress was held in Nottingham. Breadrock was invited to perform for half an hour each morning, presenting sketches on the theme of that day's discussions. The Congress provided a huge shop window for our work and invitations began to flood in afterwards. The only way these invitations could be fulfilled was by a company working full-time. Over the next few months, Murray and I had several discussions with David and the other elders at St Michael's about the project. York seemed to be the ideal base as practical support from the church households would be vital in getting it off the ground. We planned an extensive programme of work which included travelling with David as well as touring to local schools, writing and performing plays in theatres, arts centres, churches, universities and at Festivals around the country. In the first four months we produced a morality play, premièred three one-act plays by Murray, did a play by Wolf Mankowicz and wrote our first revue (a forerunner of *Colour Radio*, which won an award at the 1979 Edinburgh Festival); we also produced the first of many Christmas shows for local schools, in addition to our work with David. I doubt if we have ever worked quite as frenetically. In time, the company gained 'Equity' status which opened another door to occasional work on radio and television, though inevitably increased the financial demands upon us.

The company came into being officially on 1st September, 1977. Since then there have only been a few changes in the personnel and these have happened very gradually; most of us were already committed to working within the professional theatre before joining together to form Riding Lights. Dick Mapletoft came via Breadrock, a law degree at Cambridge and social work; Sarah Finch came from the Manchester School of Theatre; by Christmas, Geoffrey Stevenson was a permanent member and we had also been joined by Diana Lang, who came after training at the Guildhall, working with the Plymouth Theatre Royal and teaching drama for four years at Roedean. We have had five other longstanding company members—Julie Higginson (who later married Murray), Andy Harrison and on the technical and administrative side my wife Bernadette, David Heavenor and Daniel Brookes.

It was clear from the start that the company's work could not be contained entirely within the orbit of David's ministry. There was a need for us to develop forms of theatre (plays, revues and musicals) which didn't fit easily into the established pattern of missions and festivals. David wasn't blind to this development but I know that it was with some sadness that he released us from the team and with some sadness that we went. Riding Lights continued to fulfil an important role on some of the larger city-wide festivals (1977-82) and it was always the greatest joy to be back together.

Not everyone can say, 'I appeared with David Watson at the Liverpool Empire.' It *wasn't* pantomime, but on one evening we achieved it. There was a bomb scare in the Empire Theatre shortly before a youth night. Hundreds of young people were herded out on to the streets and on to the steps of St George's Hall, Encouraged by Alan Godson, a local vicar, David decided that we should improvise. He and Bishop David Sheppard preached and led prayer from inside a police van using a loud speaker system that made a noise like a vegetable shredder every few seconds; we shouted ourselves hoarse with a performance of *David and Goliath*, in which Alan Godson played the lower half of the giant, while Dick roared scornful abuse of David (not Watson) from his shoulders. Two thousand people vacated the building; two thousand five hundred went back in.

Another memorable performance of this same sketch occurred in a black church at Umlazi, during a mission which David was leading in South Africa. Five hundred people were crammed into a corrugated-iron building and had been there for two hours, singing and praying before the team arrived. The performance of the sketch took three times as long as usual. Once a line had been delivered, there was a gap while the Zulu interpreter finished laughing before he could give the translation; there was then another long gap while the audience finished laughing at the line and at the interpreter! 'Trust in God, Trust in God, Trust in God!' is the rhythmic climax to the sketch but the climax on this occasion was to see the congregation on their knees, weeping and praying for God to save Africa. Such love and spiritual reality is rarely seen and the team left feeling that they had received far more than they had given.

After all the work abroad and the travelling throughout Britain it was a relief to drop anchor occasionally in York. Once or twice St Michael's church was the setting for much larger productions, when the various creative groups in the church decided to combine their gifts for the good of the city and its huge tourist population. Murray and a composer called Christopher Norton wrote two musicals which were staged in the building: *Daniel* in 1979 and *Guy Fawkes Night* (he was baptised at St Michael's) in 1980. The church became a makeshift theatre. Black-out curtains, lighting equipment, scaffolding and staging were brought in and upwards of a hundred and fifty adults and children took part, whether acting, selling tickets, singing, playing an instrument, making costumes and banners, or building and painting huge sets which dominated the chancel. Riding Lights actors took some of the principal roles but the real value was that for once many of the congregation could be involved. It was a celebration of our corporate worship.

Four months after David's death, Riding Lights performed the latest of these large-scale productions in St Michael's for the 1984 York Festival. It was a dramatisation of *St John's Gospel* with a cast of thirteen. Over the years David saw only a few of our major productions, not least because we have never had a theatre of our own in York. Even though he related most readily to the part of our work which fitted so naturally into his own, he always encouraged the developments which we felt that God was calling us to make in a wider context. With *St. John's Gospel* the wheel had turned full circle. It was a fitting climax to seven years' work as a company which had begun with a performance of two of David's favourite sketches on a mission with him in Bradford: *The Parable of the Good Punk Rocker* and a sketch about the Cross called *The Light of the World,* after which David said he found it so easy to explain the gospel. I think those two sketches combined what David enjoyed most about our theatre—the humour and the seriousness, the raucous and the still, the way in which the Bible could be presented visually, interpreted and made compelling for the twentieth century. We had begun with our own little versions of biblical passages; *St John's Gospel* was an attempt to portray the whole text almost straight from the original. I wished that David could have been there to see it.

Chapter Six

THE PEACEMAKER

by

Cecil Kerr

Cecil Kerr is the leader and founder of the Christian
Renewal Centre in Rostrevor, Northern Ireland. The
Centre, which works towards renewal and reconciliation,
has now celebrated its tenth anniversary.

I had the great joy of knowing and working with David Watson over a period of ten years. In that time God used his ministry of evangelism, renewal and reconciliation all over the world, but his forthright exposition of the biblical teaching on reconcilation has been particularly relevant in Ireland.

Many thousands of people in Ireland, North and South, remember David with profound thankfulness for his life and ministry. Although he had travelled in many parts of the world, Ireland held a special place in his affections; he visited the North six times for major campaigns and Dublin on three occasions. Indeed the last major mission which David led was held in Belfast and Dublin in November 1983, and we shall never forget the powerful and prophetic message which he gave during that week. Even though he was then very weak in body, his proclamation of the gospel carried more conviction, and he spoke with greater urgency to our situation. He felt deeply the wounds of the divisions in the Body of Christ in Ireland. And yet he did not despair—he said to me that November, 'In Ireland you know where the real battle is. You sense the reality of the power of evil but you also see clearly the mighty power of good revealed in so many lives.'

David's teaching on the subject of reconcilation had been hammered out on the anvil of his own experience and he often described his pilgrimage from a very narrow and bigoted theological position to a clearer understanding of the meaning of the unity of all believers in the Body of Christ. One might use the two bars of the Cross as an illustration of this point. The vertical bar reminds us that we are reconciled to God in Christ, through repentance and faith, and the horizontal tells us that through that act of God's love we are reconciled with all those who kneel there with us—whatever their race or religious background might be.

Because David allowed God to deal so deeply with his own attitudes and prejudices he was free to minister that deliverance to others, and people from a wide variety of Christian traditions attended the meetings at which he spoke. However difficult the struggle might be, we were all made aware that any obstacles to fellowship within the Body of Christ must become urgent concerns for us in such a divided community.

The Church of Ireland diocese of Down and Dromore, which embraces a large part of Belfast and stretches down to the border with the Republic, had a special relationship with David. In 1970 when Bishop George Quin was appointed to lead the diocese, there was no doubt in his mind that spiritual renewal should be the top priority in his episcopate. The relevant worship and meaningful sharing of ministry in an ordered Anglican setting, such as that of St Michael-le-Belfrey, appealed to many of those clergy and lay people in the diocese who were eagerly responding to the Bishop's call for renewal. As a result, large parties of clergy and lay people made the journey to York and brought back a new vision of what God would do in the Church of Ireland; the visit of David and his team to Belfast Cathedral and other centres also had a powerful effect. I am sure it is no accident that during the decade of renewal under Bishop Quin the diocese of Down and Dromore has produced almost as many ordinands as the rest of the Church of Ireland put together!

The Church of Ireland was not alone in recognising the stimulating model provided by the spiritual growth at St Michael's. Invitations for David and his team to minister also came from other denominations. The newly-built Forum in Antrim provided an ideal setting for the presentation of drama and dance which accompanied David's clear biblical teaching, and Fisherwick Presbyterian Church also hosted a special mission.

One of the most moving events in which David participated was undoubtedly the Third National Conference on Charismatic Renewal at the Royal Dublin Society Showground in September 1976. I have no doubt that the experience of this Conference strengthened David's growing conviction of the importance of reconciliation as a central theme of his ministry. Anne accompanied David to the Conference, and it was a great inspiration to see how God used them together. Anne was invited to join the platform party and at least one of the words of prophecy came through her ministry. I recall the obvious joy that it gave them both to share in this work for God.

In the winter of 1982 David and I were together at a prayer meeting in the House of Lords at Westminster, and we talked then about another visit to Ireland. David expressed excitement at the prospect, but when we had the sad news of his illness early in the year, we wondered whether he would be able to come. Then, in the summer of 1983, my wife and I were in York for a brief visit, and it happened that David and Anne were visiting St Michael's on the same day. 'How about our visit to Ireland?' said David, and so arrangements were made for him to come over in November.

That visit with the team was to be David's last major outreach, and it made a powerful impact on Ireland, North and South. We all knew the courageous and faith-filled battle he was fighting against cancer yet, as a dying man preaching to dying men, he brought a strong message of hope. The visit was during the week after the terrible tragedy when IRA gunmen had burst into a little Pentecostal Church on the border, killing three elders and seriously wounding many other men, women and children: an appropriate moment for David and his team to bring the message which they so movingly shared in word and song and in dance and music.

A large Roman Catholic church in the suburbs of Dublin was filled to capacity for an unforgettable festival of praise. Seven hard years of suffering had passed since the great meeting at the Dublin showground and many had died in the violence, but that night there was born in the hearts of many a new determination to move forward in God's purpose 'to unite all things in heaven and earth in Christ'. On a cold November evening Church House, in the centre of Belfast, was filled with two thousand people from the Shankill and the Falls and from many other parts of Northern Ireland. Clergy and leaders from different denominations found their lives and ministries profoundly affected by David's work and life as they heard him speak.

As we travelled together in Ireland, David and I had talked about the lessons the Lord was teaching us for his whole Body, the Church, through the terrible disease of cancer. You could have a heard a pin drop in that vast audience in Belfast, as David related the effects of cancer in the human body to the effects of selfish indifference and divisions in the Church of Jesus Christ. As death approached for David, it seemed as if the Lord was appealing through him to the whole Church to fulfil

Christ's longing 'that they may all be one'.

Thousands all over Ireland had been praying for David and Anne and their family, and the news of David's death came as a great shock; but it was coupled with profound thanksgiving for God's gift in him to the whole Church. A most moving and inspiring service of thanksgiving was held in Fisherwick Presbyterian Church, Belfast, on Tuesday 10th April 1984. The service was arranged by the Rev Ken Newell, a Presbyterian minister, and drew together the three major themes of David's ministry: evangelism, spiritual renewal and reconciliation. Taking part were two Presbyterian ministers, a Methodist minister, a friend of David's from the Belfast YMCA, a Roman Catholic priest from Dublin, Bishop George Quin, and myself.

One of the songs which drew us all together expressed well the prayer that I know was often on David's heart, not only for Ireland but for the Church in all the world:

> Give us a fresh understanding
> Of brotherly love that is real,
> Let there be love shared among us,
> Let there be love!

Words and music by Dave Bilbrough. Copyright © 1979 Thankyou Music, P.O. Box 75, Eastbourne BN23 6NW. Used by permission.

Chapter Seven

LOVE AT ALL COSTS

by

David Armstrong

David Armstrong, Presbyterian minister in Limavady, Northern Ireland, was greatly influenced by the ministry of David Watson, whom he first met in 1977. He is chaplain at Magilligan Prison, and is married with four children.

Shortly after hearing about the Rev David Watson from a friend, I noticed an article on him in a magazine. To my mind, a few heresies were abroad. For a start he did not seem to know that one was baptised with the Spirit at conversion—there he was in the article, telling readers of his conversion at Cambridge and a baptism in the Spirit years later when preaching through the beatitudes! Then he spoke of miracles. Did he not know that the day of miracles finished with the apostles? Next he actually believed in speaking in tongues! And the suggestion that Roman Catholics 'in love with Christ' might be Christians seemed to me a major deviation. Lastly, he recommended the use of drama and movement in church worship—and my Ulster Presbyterian mind had quite enough. If the magazine article was accurate, and I had no reason to believe it wasn't, David Watson was a big disappointment.

However those pages did leave questions in my mind and these lingered during my final years at college. I was then appointed assistant at First Carrickfergus Presbyterian Church, some ten miles along the Antrim coast from Belfast. Surely there must be some mistake, I thought! I was strong in my fundamentalism and yet I had been placed with the Rev Ronnie Craig, a former

Irish rugby full-back, very sympathetic to Dr William Barclay of Scotland and therefore not solidly orthodox. The first six months were awkward and I could see that my boss found my presence quite disconcerting; our relationship was polite but not deep.

In the *Belfast Telegraph* one Saturday evening, there appeared an advertisement announcing a mission in St Anne's Cathedral, Belfast. The missioner was none other than David Watson. I was free on the Tuesday evening of the mission and decided to go along—he was speaking to the non-Christians and if they were going to be converted, all well and good! After all, I thought, he would be leaving the following week and we would not have to put up with his strange ideas for long!

The first surprise I had when I arrived in St Anne's was the very large crowd there to greet this English preacher. But there was more for which I was not prepared. David Watson spoke to Christians in his sermon; he sought to explain new life in Christ to those in Northern Ireland who said they were already converted. He was even preaching to someone beginning his ministry; he was preaching to someone like myself. What a challenge was brought to the Christians of Belfast during that mission! He asked us whether if we *were* full of the Holy Spirit, the fruit of the Spirit was evident in our lives. Where were the love, joy and peace? He was not asking us to change our doctrine but to change our *attitude* towards those who held different doctrine. 'Do you listen to what Roman Catholics say, or do you listen to what you *think* they say?' Was Christ to be seen in us? 'From your eyes he beckons me and from your heart his love is shed, until I lose sight of you and see the Christ instead'. Did we come to church to worship Christ from the neck up? I had to ask myself the question, 'Did I come to church to really worship?!' This needed answering bearing in mind that the first question in my Presbyterian catechism was 'What is man's chief end?' The reply that is on the lips of all our children is that 'man's chief end is to glorify God and enjoy him forever!'

I could now see that with David Watson's excellent communicative style, his direct and well-researched message and his lively team it was no wonder at all that young people at his church in York looked forward to worship. The team when they spoke, sang or danced, portrayed the joy of those with resurrection life. It was not modernistic oversimplification; what we saw was as old as the New Testament itself. Now I knew what John meant when he said the Word was made flesh and dwelt among us and we *beheld*. Surely in our country what was needed was that our faith should be put into action. David asked us if we had fully opened our lives to the Holy Spirit and used the simple illustration of the glove. The hand halfway into the glove was capable of nothing; only when it was fully inside did it have the power to do useful things.

Before the closing hymn at the Thursday night meeting, David led the congregation in prayer. It was a prayer of turning to God, rededication to Christ and request to be filled with the Holy Spirit. David had told his hearers that the aim of being filled with the Holy Spirit was not primarily that we may *feel* better but that God would make us more *useful* in his service. That night I handed my life over to God completely and asked him to fill every area of my life with his Holy Spirit.

I prayed that the Lord might make me useful to others and that the newness of life might be seen in me. On the way home June, my wife, could see that I had met my God in a new way and I realised that she too had made that prayer of commitment. Next morning I met my boss Ronnie Craig at our 'Morning Watch' service, designed for shoppers, and told him of my experience with Christ at the service the previous evening in Belfast. He was pleased for me, although I am sure that he decided to wait and see how this was going to work out in everyday parish life.

Sunday morning worship was certainly 'worship with a difference'! I no longer wanted to be a great preacher, but rather to preach a great Saviour. One of the elders was the first to spot the difference: he detected in my attitude to the Scriptures that God had filled me with his Holy Spirit. Encouragement also came from a minister in nearby Ballyclare, who had experienced God afresh at a Renewal Service in Rostrevor, County Down. In his front room we talked about what had happened to us. We had not received a frothy new faith that burst at the first sign of difficulty, but rather a resilient trust which sought not to avoid difficulties but to go through them.

A few weeks later, I felt that I should write to David and let him know what an encouragement his mission had been to June and me. Part of that letter is included in *You Are My God.* A few days later we received a big surprise. 'Come to York!' David said. 'Get permission from Ronnie Craig, arrive in time for a Thursday fellowship and stay until Monday morning!' June and I could not believe it. This busy man who had helped us already was prepared, even amidst a busy schedule, to help us still more. Ronnie Craig readily agreed with the suggestion and we were soon on our way to York.

What an abundance of life was evident in the people at that Thursday evening fellowship meeting! They were so warm, friendly and loving, and we received great blessing and encouragement from them. The Body of Christ was functioning through the life of his people who gathered there for worship; the gifts of the Spirit were in operation but never was there a lack of self-control. All that was done was orderly, but the breath of life was felt in power.

The Friday was spent largely in the study where we heard David get to grips with matters theological concerning the first four chapters in Acts. On Saturday, he was going with some of the team to Woodhall, not far from Leeds, to conduct worship for Monsignor Michael Buckley. He asked us to go with him and part of the team of singers. Before we set out in the Land-rover, David did warn us that Michael was a Roman Catholic priest and that he was going that afternoon to address a gathering largely composed of Roman Catholics. June and I took our seats and worship commenced. Sitting all around us were people eagerly praising Christ. To see and hear those people sing 'Father, we adore you' caused me to breathe a sigh and say 'If only a quarter of our Protestant churches back home were able to praise God like this then perhaps our problems would disappear!' Roman Catholic people testified to the reality of the living presence of Christ within them in a way that I thought only possible in the Protestant tradition. Prayer was spontaneous with little pause, and even when there was a pause it too was meaningful. To meet Michael Buckley was a joy too, and twenty minutes with him caused us to stretch forward into new realms of praise. His love for Christ was genuine and strong.

All this was to be more significant when we returned home to Carrickfergus. A new priest had arrived a few miles away in Greenisland. He was made welcome in our home and within moments we realised that although we differed in certain theological aspects we shared a strong and sincere love for the Lord Jesus. We were soon to be joined by the Anglican minister and the Methodist minister. One Saturday night in the month was set aside for a joint praise gathering and these will always stand out in my memory. You may say that such gatherings are not unusual on the English mainland, but don't forget this is Northern Ireland! Ronnie Craig was pleased to learn of these meetings and gave them his full blessing.

The Youth Fellowship in the congregation greatly flourished. Four young people responded to an invitation to come to our home for worship; a month or two later nearly forty young people were coming and the meetings moved to the church hall. These young people had come with a profound longing to seek God and were determinded to praise him in the power of the Spirit. June and I look back on those days with much joy. How humbled we feel that God chose to use us in bringing these young people to Christ and then to watch them grow, evangelising through drama, praising God in tongues, and in every way leading Christ-like lives. They were ready to show much love to those Roman Catholics who also had a deep love for Christ and a desire to praise him. June and I never cease to thank God for the Carrickfergus youth.

Some months after St Anne's mission in Belfast I suggested that we might arrange for a similar mission in Carrickfergus, led by David Watson. I had by that time a different relationship with Ronnie Craig; we had a strong Christian love for one another and a trust that had now greatly matured. Since God had visited my heart, breaking down the coldness that was there, this newness of life was reflected in my attitudes to others. After much prayer David agreed to come for a week, and it was with great expectation that I set off for York with Dr Craig to introduce them to each other. Immediately there was a strong bond between David and Ronnie Craig.

We had a great series of meetings in Carrickfergus with David and the team despite a difficult start. Unfortunately there was almost a street cabaret before the opening meeting when a good number of protesters, many from outside Carrickfergus, arrived outside to voice their objection to David's attitude to Roman Catholics. However they had a perfect right to protest, just as David had every right to love Roman Catholics.

Our church was much helped by those meetings; shining through each one was David's intense love for the Irish and his deep desire that renewal would help bring reconciliation to the province. Ronnie Craig confessed that these services had made a great impact on him, and a few years later the Presbyterian Church throughout Ireland were to greatly honour him by appointing him as Moderator. He had no hesitation in moving amongst the Roman Catholics of our land, north and south, pleading that everyone might be reconciled through Christ.

Ronnie Craig's interest in sport prompted me to take on the post of chaplain to the East Belfast soccer team Glentoran. When I arrived the whole team were Protestant and it seemed that the supporters wanted it that way. However the position has changed and we have five Roman Catholics on the now non-sectarian team. The Roman Catholic players accept me as a friend and it is an honour to be their chaplain.

After five years at Carrickfergus, we moved to Limavady in County Londonderry. The population of Limavady is about 55% Protestant and there is tension between the Protestant and the Catholic claims for superiority. Carrickfergus was roughly 90% Protestant so Protestants did not feel that their dominance was threatened. When we arrived the local paper carried an attack on me—basically for being a friend of David Watson. I was said to be a Romaniser and compromiser, and perhaps one or two other things! The attacks came from the Free Presbyterian Church in Limavady. Although I would differ from them on certain political as well as ecclesiastical matters I reserve them the right to speak their mind. One thing I never do is to seek to preach sermons back; my love must also go out to them even though we may have our differences.

One fateful Sunday evening a few months after my arrival an enormous explosion was heard over all Limavady. I quickly realised that the site of the explosion was the new Catholic church next door to ours, and on arrival I could see against the darkened sky a pall of smoke coming from where the roof had been. Our church was ankle-deep in glass, and I stood there as the police arrived, listening to the gathering crowd. Hardened Protestants were saying, 'The Roman Catholics did that themselves to get insurance claims'; I was convinced that it was the work of a Protestant paramilitary group. I spoke on the media telling Catholics throughout the province that I was sincerely sorry at what had happened to their building. Thankfully many Limavady Protestants supported me, but there were those who insisted I was wrong to feel disappointed that a Catholic building had been attacked in such a way. David Watson prayed earnestly for me during those days.

When repair of the Roman Catholic church was completed I received an invitation to the opening service conducted by the Roman Catholic Bishop of Londonderry, Dr Edward Daley and I had little hesitation in accepting as I wished to show neighbourly friendship and courtesy. Some were angry and we did feel the hurt, but we know that if there is to be healing and reconciliation in this divided land *someone* has to cross the threshold at rural parish level. A week or so later deep tragedy hit our district. There was a massive bomb explosion at the Drop Inn Well Disco resulting in seventeen deaths. The Provisional IRA claimed responsibility. Imagine how I felt when I walked through the town that day. People looked at me as if to say, 'Roman Catholics did this, and *you* went to their church opening!' I longed for people to realise that the whole Roman Catholic community cannot be blamed for the actions of a few. The day of that disaster is still vivid in my memory and I pray that one day soon such dreadful actions and wanton suffering will come to an end.

Two years ago I was appointed chaplain at Magilligan Prison, County Londonderry, where I have been given full scope to work for reconciliation. A terrorist coming to Christ needs not only to be reconciled to God but also to his fellow man, and I have witnessed Republican and Protestant prisoners embrace one another in Christ. David Watson was also very encouraged during his illness by letters from Liam McCloskey who had been on hunger strike as a Republican for fifty-five days, and for three and a half years had fouled his cell. Both he and Jimmy Gibson, a Protestant terrorist from Belfast, accepted Christ whilst in prison. It was heartwarming to watch them studying the Bible together, and now that they have been released they help to lead services of evange-lism and reconciliation.

Encouragements such as this have caused me to stay in Ulster despite the problems, tears and threats. David Watson advised me to remain here and indeed my whole ministry has changed under his influence. With a new confidence of the presence of God and an assurance that all things *will* work together for good for those who love God I have been given a new longing for reconciliation. It's not just a case of peace at any price, but rather love at all costs.

Chapter Eight

ST MICHAEL-LE-BELFREY

by

John Poulton

Canon John Poulton is the Vice-Dean of Norwich Cathedral. In the course of his work for the Archbishops' Council on Evangelism (ACE) he made a study of St Michael's in 1977.

At the end of 1977 David Watson asked me to take a look at St Michael-le-Belfrey with a team of friends. For a number of years the Archbishops' Council on Evangelism (ACE), for which I was then working, had been doing a series of 'parish studies'. We had come to see that the very fact of outsiders asking questions was likely to cause change and that nothing stayed the same long enough to be still there when your report was written; therefore 'action-research' was the name of the game.

None of us who were involved in that exercise will ever forget the warm and hospitable response to our probing presence; neither will we forget how genuinely everyone joined in the exercise, in honesty and in humility. It cannot have been easy to do so openly, nor to live with the processes of new thinking and change which it began. I felt that this love, honesty and humility—the willingness to accept the pain of changing—were but further proof, if proof were needed, of the presence of God's Spirit and the congregation's desire to live by him.

It is not necessary in this book to recall everything which we found there; others have given their impressions of various aspects of the work. Let me come straight to the heart of things with what I wrote at the time about an evening service at St Michael-le-Belfrey.

David Watson preaches. Not only the service, but the whole life of the congregation hinges upon this fact.

He is a crisp, careful preacher. Into every sermon goes all his life before it—but also a hefty period of specific preparation. His illustrations are from personal experience, or from his wide reading, or from the newspaper. They are appropriate. He is not the preacher who puts in anecdotes for their own sake. David's particular anecdote comes where it must be. There are no dramatics, little rhetoric. The basic style is plain teaching. That the Spirit is in it you do not doubt. There is no attempt to work up an atmosphere.

Whichever service you happen to choose, you are likely to arrive for a sermon which comes half-way through some pre-announced series. Over the years hundreds of such sermons have been delivered, and are still available on cassette. There is a worldwide postal ministry using these cassettes. The service you are there for will later be listened to by missionaries in Thailand and pensioners in Torquay.

Why is the atmosphere so electric then? Prayer is one clue: David's own prayer life. The prayers of the congregation on Thursday evenings (when 150-200 come for the prayer-meeting); in area groups; and in their homes. Prayer is obviously the warp and woof of the whole process, prayer that expects God's answers, and knows that he expects this of his children. Beyond that, it hardly needs saying that David Watson is a gifted person! He can communicate effectively. He is a talented evangelist and expositor. Moreover, he knows his people so well that he speaks convincingly to them, as part of the one Body which is doing the one job together.

Of course there are gaps. Though David does regularly preach on the need for Christian commitment to neighbourhood and community and to global concerns, he tends to be heard within the narrower framework of personal religion. Commitment to the world in need via Tear Fund, for example, is likely to be heard in terms of evangelism, preaching overseas for conversions. Though the Good Samaritan role will be fulfilled in some of the things Tear Fund does, there is the danger that these will be seen as a means to that end. Responsibility in the city is likely to be heard as a 'watchman' responsibility to make known the gospel to those who else may perish without Christ.

Tonight David is preaching about eldership because he will shortly appoint for a three-year stint a new group of elders. He explains from the pastoral epistles why he believes the biblical pattern to be that names should be sent in, but that the appointments should be made by him, not by election. He therefore describes the qualities of those to be appointed and leads the congregation in prayer for wisdom in discerning them.

For the Holy Communion people stream up to the front of the church. On the raised dais, where a liturgical dance has just sought to express the worship of God's people, elders stand to help in the administration. Whilst all receive the bread and wine, some people also are there for the laying-on of hands, or for prayer. It is a holy time, everybody very much aware of God's presence in their midst. There are many smiles, a few hugs, clearly a time of focus for the fellowship that is lived out in a hundred different ways during the week.

The corporate nature of the evangelistic impact of St Michael-le-Belfrey is witnessed to by many who have come to a personal relationship with Christ there, and from it we learn one of the greatest lessons of David Watson's ministry. When at some point in the service David reminds those who have never come to Christ that he is waiting for their response, one sees that he is only putting into words that which is already evident in the lives *and attitudes of those who are worshipping God together.*

Crowds hang on after the service ends. There is a bookstall at the back where some congregate, and where there is a good trade. Many stay in church with their friends. Newcomers are welcomed. David and the elders continue their personal talking with individuals. Some, somewhere, are presumably counting collections for the day, which average £500, but that really is a detail.

Already from that account of one Sunday evening, a clear picture emerges. David Watson was the presbyter, leader of the family of the local church. Around him he gathered those personally gifted people to share in ministry. It was their job to develop a proper care for the members of the whole congregation.

They were almost all professional men earning their living in the city during the week. One or two were 'full-timers', one was running the youth centre for the 'unattached' (why do the sociologists invent such ugly and dehumanising terms for people?). One was an officially appointed lay pastor to the congregation, spending much of his time visiting in homes and in hospitals, counselling, encouraging, evangelising.

All the elders were responsible for several area groups of St Michael people. Those groups had their own leaders and when the system was working properly, the plan was for the elders to support and encourage those leaders. However, some of the groups had grown to fifty people which was not a group, but more of a public meeting! So there were problems.

The vision was there right enough. The elders were not only responsible within the structure for the supervision of area group leaders: they were known and respected and loved members of the congregation being consulted by members themselves. It was not a rigid system but felt warm and human. Nevertheless the system

123

was not always efficient. Fish slipped regularly through the nets. As in any other large congregation, people would sometimes say 'we never see anyone'.

Some of the married elders, who seemed to be out every night of the week, would feel depressed; their families might have put it even stronger! David and the people of St Michael-le-Belfrey did not in the end discover all the answers to the question: How do you pastor a thousand people satisfactorily and stay relaxed in the process?

So central to David's ministry in York was this question of shared leadership that I want to pursue it a little further. David himself wrote of the beginnings of the use of eldership:

'As the congregation grew in size (from about a dozen originally), the need to share the leadership and the pastoral work of the church became more and more obvious. In true biblical style, there was murmuring that various people were being neglected! After some specific teaching about shared leadership and ministry, I asked the congregation to pray about the matter for a week and then to submit to me the names of up to seven men, "full of faith and of the Holy Spirit", who were obviously being used by God in pastoral counselling. Naturally I prayed very much during the week as well; and the names submitted to me in writing were identical with the ones I had personally chosen, which was a wonderful confirmation of God's guidance. This was not an election. The church is not a democracy, and the elders have always been ultimately by appointment, although checked by the congregation in the way described.'

The elders, later increased in number and responsibility, met regularly for prayer and discussion with David. He made it a priority to keep a constant link with the other leaders, believing that the harmony of a church depends on the harmony of its leadership. All decisions at the elders' meetings were unanimous. If there was at first a difference of opinion, they waited until they had reached an agreed policy. David submitted to the elders the invitations to preach or lead missions elsewhere, and therefore felt whenever he went from St Michael-le-Belfrey, say on a mission, that he was 'sent out' with the full approval of the elders, who often laid hands on him and prayed for him in the presence of the congregation.

There are I think three comments to be made on this style of congregational leadership which do not detract from its value but which question some of the false assumptions which have been placed upon it by people elsewhere.

Firstly, what was happening was not so much 'shared leadership' as 'group leadership' in the sense that the members of the congregation did not themselves 'share' in decision-making. This was the business of the elders' group.

Secondly, David's own position was not what is implied in the phrase *primus inter pares*. Although in a superficial way his role might have looked like that of one elder among others, he had the sole right of appointing and dismissing them, however much he might consult along the way. His way of management was that of an authority structure, moving from charismatic leadership to a classical or pyramidic headship. He was thus verbally committed, by his understanding of the pastoral epistles in particular, to a systemic or shared leadership, while events (and perhaps his own personality as well) moved in an opposite direction. I have used the word 'authority' above, but that word and 'power' were avoided in discussion at St Michael's, being substituted by 'serving and caring roles'. Semantics do not, however, alter facts.

I can illustrate what I mean in an apparently simple matter like the raising of agenda in elders' meetings.

David would come to these meetings with a list of points he had accumulated during the week. As a result there was seldom time for others to raise their own agenda after he had finished his. This was a form of leadership which in other organisations is used in directive patterns rather than in enabling or facilitating styles of leadership. There are limits therefore to the extent to which we may really call David's style a *shared* pattern of leadership.

Thirdly—and this is really only an Anglican footnote —once the eldership system had come into operation, the PCC became much more a routine administrative group, deprived of the opportunity to comment creatively upon matters of strategy. The PCC and Standing Committee (the elected and representative organ of the local church under Synodical Government in the Church of England) took on a subsidiary role. It was probably significant that the electoral figures for the church did not seem to have been kept adequately, and very little importance was placed upon electoral roll membership. In other words, the voting rights of the laity at annual meetings were simply not significant. A parish development that seemed to be one of 'shared leadership' proved to have been at the expense of member-responsibility.

We can follow this line of thought through as we come to look at how the area groups worked. Prior to 1972, several house groups, Bible study groups, prayer groups, and evangelistic house meetings had been held. But area groups as such were started in October 1973 following discussion in the Church Council and a congregational teach-in and discussion. Eighteen groups were formed by the eighteen selected leaders appointed by David Watson himself, the number stayed constant until 1977 when it increased to twenty. It may be fair to describe the congregation as having a multi-centred organisation or a 'cellular sub-structure', but the growth of St Michael-le-Belfrey was certainly not by means of cellular multiplication. A series of fairly static units were organised in 1973 and had remained fairly much the same ever since; their capacity did not expand to match the massive rises in attendance at church.

Some members wanted more freedom to participate, more share in leadership, and more social interaction. Indeed when the groups had a nominal roll of up to fifty members (and attendances of only about a third of that number), the pressure for division into smaller groups grew strong. However this cellular development did not happen.

During the ACE study, people in the area groups were asked to comment on changes they desired. People in larger groups wanted a less formal programme. People in smaller groups wanted a more formal programme. Both reflected the same situation. By and large, leaders of the house groups were appointed by David Watson and the elders and chosen for their spiritual maturity rather than for any particular charisma in small group leadership. They tended therefore to do the obvious thing, reflecting the style of David and the elders in church and in the Thursday evening fellowship meetings. In the larger groups they behaved as if they were in St Cuthbert's on a Thursday, talking down to the people. In the smaller groups where this obviously could not be done, they concentrated on 'fellowship' and sometimes lost the sense of direction and purpose.

One member of the ACE team, herself a skilled leader in small group leadership and observation, commented:

> Even though human beings spend most of their lives in groups, the systematic study of group process and its impacts upon group productivity are not taught at St Michael's. Several leaders said in some way that they would like help in this area.

In important parallel, this disquiet at the area group leaders' level reflects the techniques used in other leadership teaching situations in St Michael's. When elders are themselves taught in a basically hierarchical environment, it is not surprising when the same methods are used lower down the ladder. Leaders control groups; they see to it that meetings cover *their* agenda and reach the ends *they* envisage. This may encourage respect and admiration, strengthening self-images. However the price is paid in stress and frustrations, which are outweighed only by the strong need for belonging and self-identity.

Since the central need that the area groups seek to meet is that of fellowship, it is hardly surprising that the groups have not played a particularly significant role in evangelism in St Michael's. Occasionally area groups have held their own evangelistic events, but this is not what their members have seen them as being for. They have an essentially caring, supportive, teaching function within the congregation. Let it be said too, that this accords with the strategy as determined by the church. There is a real area of tension here with the area groups representing quite accurately the determination not to split the St Michael's family, and the equally strong desire for fellowship face-to-face in small groups within 'too large a congregation.'

It will be apparent in other chapters of this book that one of the remarkable features of the life of St Michael-le-Belfrey in David Watson's time was the 'households'. These were mini-communities within the large community, and in some respects were translating a long Catholic experience in the Religious Orders into modern, lay, 'secular' terms. These households supported various full-time people in ministry, including particularly those responsible for music and drama. They were the expression within St Michael's of those aspects of fellowship which, in the early church, caused Christians to 'have all things in common'. They were therefore the places where the congregation took its commitment to 'poverty' and 'love' most seriously. Undoubtedly they extended very considerably the forms and quantity of ministry on offer to and by the whole congregation.

One can but salute those who, with the best of motivations and the deepest devotion, entered upon this experience of close community. Some made considerable financial sacrifices to join; some experienced the heightening of family strains which become highlighted when space and privacy are sacrificed; many found their personal weaknesses or inadequacies thrown into stark relief by twenty-four hour exposure to others. Tremendous awareness of loss, guilt, anger, feelings of being trapped, or having taken irrevocable and probably wrong steps, are all written into this sort of community experience.

With the very strong stress on 'one family' at St Michael's, one can discern how in a deep sense the households were used, albeit unconsciously, as the areas in which the whole congregation allowed the more difficult, negative, emotional facets of fellowship and maturation to be worked out. It became almost a priestly role as they accepted suffering on behalf of the rest of the congregation.

This was accentuated in a congregation in which conflict and argument and growth through confrontation and openness were normally discouraged or avoided. Almost as a theological principle, negative forces were suspect, and peace and harmony unquestioningly taken to be the norms the Spirit requires of his people. The feel of David's own ministry and leadership was one in which all the stress was on love, and confrontation was not to be expected or countenanced, since, theologically speaking, 'we are one in the Spirit, we are one in the Lord'.

The plain truth is, however, that in any human grouping, grief, conflict and loss have all to be coped with in one way or another. Perhaps the St Michael way was to push these back into the experience of those in the households, rather than have them manifested in embarrassingly public situations. To make this point specific, when David Watson went out on one of his major evangelistic missions, he would take with him the drama, music and leadership teams, leaving the households bereft and having to handle the sense of loss, some of them virtually emptied for the time of the mission.

Questions such as these could only be raised responsibly against the whole background of what was and is a healthy, joyful and open fellowship at St Michael-le-Belfrey.

The whole of that fellowship has been marked from the very beginnings by prayer. The story of the way Anne and David prayed renewal into the life of St Cuthbert's with that faithful band of supporters at the beginning has often been recounted. Throughout his ministry at St Cuthbert's, David always stressed the importance of prayer in matters both big and small, spiritual and material.

The mid-week meeting in those early days started in one room in the Rectory, gradually expanding to several rooms and the stairs relayed by sound relay, and eventually moved to the church annexe, and finally to the church itself. Something like two hundred people would come to this meeting, which consisted of a Bible reading and exposition and then a time of open prayer and praise. In addition there were regular half-nights of prayer focusing on the guest services and on the work of the Christian coffee bar ('Catacombs') with which the church was closely involved. During these times of prayer there was also much praise and worship and ministry of the gifts of the Spirit (particularly 'prophecy', but occasionally also 'tongues' and 'interpretation'). When David was away on a university mission or elsewhere, the mid-week times of prayer naturally concentrated on the work to which God had called him, and the whole congregation felt involved in his wider ministry. During a prolonged mission or series of missions a close link was often maintained through taped reports. In addition to these larger prayer-meetings there were a number of smaller prayer groups meeting in homes throughout the week and a telephone prayer chain whereby a large number of people could be linked in prayer in a very short time when any specially urgent need arose.

As with my earlier comments on area groups, I have to say here that these church-based periods of prayer involved, with all their sincerity, a given style which again was handed down from the top. Perhaps more important is the fact that many many Christians were developing within an atmosphere which really believed God answers prayer and that he wills for his children the exercise of asking him. When one experienced this within the dance group or the drama company in their rehearsing time, beginning with a time of prayer and honest personal sharing together, one knew one was in the presence of a very deep dimension of Christian reality.

The other new dimension which marked David's developing ministry in York was the realisation that living worship discloses God as much as preaching. There was no doubt about the good feel of the large Sunday evening services. There was a similar rightness about family worship in the mornings, attended particularly by younger members of the congregation. But, morning or evening, the clergy, elders and articulate lay people would all say that the whole event communicated, and not *just* the talk or the sermon. David himself used to say that once upon a time an evangelist would 'use' music and worship as an approach to the spoken message.

What he learned in York and what I believe the whole Church has to pick up in the television age, was the fact that where God's Spirit is in worship, the proclaiming of Christ has *already* begun with power.

Some of us only realised fully the extent to which David Watson's style of 'embodied' evangelism spoke to our times and our needs when Mission England brought Billy Graham here in 1984. Here, for all its impact and worth, was an approach to evangelism which concentrated upon the evangelist himself at the expense of the church side of commitment and experience.

David was the first to acknowledge that the preaching or teaching ministry was absolutely essential. What was so important about his evangelistic preaching, however, was the way in which, whether at home in York or away on missions, David Watson was never merely David Watson. His words were always within the context of God's people who were enjoying worshipping him together. What came across was the sheer weight of testimony upholding the Word preached, by the Word received, believed in and being lived by so many happy but ordinary people who were themselves part of the proclaiming, whether they were participating up-front or as members of the congregation.

No one congregation and no one minister gets it all right at the same time. St Michael-le-Belfrey and David Watson missions were truly marked by an incarnational style. On the other hand, the preaching and activity in York seemed too much to be taken up by and bounded by church activity. To listen to notices in church on Sunday might well give the impression of a warm and enthusiastic people offering an out-of-the-world, seven-days-a-week life. But too easily church fellowship can become a tabernacle built on the Mount of Transfiguration.

St Michael-le-Belfrey never had any particular impact

on its immediate parish (small though that was) nor did David seem to stress the need for Christian involvement in the life of the city or of secular activity. An eclectic congregation, St Michael's did not have any measurable impact outside the professional and student worlds which cheerfully supported it. There were those who felt that St Michael's could at least have made the effort to contact the skilled artisans in York, but somehow there were always invisible barriers being drawn.

These barriers work in peculiar ways in a congregation. The ACE parish studies to which I have referred led us to the conclusion that there are 'comfortable' numbers for doing different things, or for different stages in the life of a congregation. Translating this into David's ministry, one sees that at a certain stage in 1972 St Cuthbert's became so obviously too small (even with closed-circuit television relays) that something had to be done about it. Evening services were transferred to St Michael-le-Belfrey in the shadow of the Minster. By that point, however, numbers coming on Sunday evening had already begun to decline—people were having to come earlier and earlier to get a seat at all. A group reacts to becoming uncomfortable by reducing the pressure on space. No one decides this: it just happens. As David Wasdell has put it, traditionally structured congregations have a self-limiting pattern of growth. A congregation increases

> to the point at which, because of dissatisfaction and break-down of its inner community resources, people start to leave just as fast as others are added. The church on the plateau is a human group whose needs for belonging and significance have stretched to the point of disintegration.

At St Cuthbert's, the congregation answered the problem by moving out into larger premises. This only delayed somewhat the need to find deeper solutions. Faced shortly afterwards with the challenge of a much bigger place to fill at St Michael-le-Belfrey the congregation shifted again into top gear and the attendance graph took off (together with the financial giving) until once again the excitement of a challenge gave way to the plateau sickness. Discomfort was being experienced and decline imperceptibly began to set in. Whilst people like to be part of a big show, at the same time they are looking for a fellowship which cannot be found in the larger group.

We have seen already that this was partly answered by the setting up of area house groups, but that these did not deal well with the important matter of 'comfortable' size. All relevant studies suggest eight to twelve as the optimum size for groups for personal growth and Christian maturation. The St Michael's groups were not small enough to function in this way; neither were they being run as house churches, or embryo new congregations. Inevitably they fell between two stools. The stress remained on the family of St Michael's whilst the strictly controlled groups struggled to deal with the large numbers who were looking for fellowship within the congregation.

I have myself little doubt that when in time it is possible to stand back from David Watson's ministry and to assess what it was saying to the Church at the time, one of the important factors will be his encouragement of dance and drama and orchestra and different styles of music, all within the one ministry and style of worship. Christians in the television age are still finding it very hard to act as if they believed that man does *not* learn by words alone. David knew this and practised it. He did not always carry everybody with him as he gave freedom to those who were

134

experimenting in the arts. This was one area where there really could be controversy in St Michael's. Yet at the time there were so few congregations as free to experiment in those other forms, although dance, movement and drama are the building blocks of the television age, and the media whereby most adult mass communication now takes place. When the object is the communication of Christ to today's world, experiments in the most effective blending of dance, music, movement, drama, participation in liturgical prayer and preaching and everyday witness, become critical.

It is fascinating, observing the modern scene, to realise how very few have achieved what David Watson achieved. So closely united in the Spirit were he and his teams that the proclamation by David never appeared to be anything but as a part of the whole, a seamless robe. All too often a powerful piece of drama upstages a subsequent preaching, or a beautiful piece of music is not allowed to have its own impact before it is submerged in words. David was a master of getting the balance right.

Let me then try the impossible task of summing this up. Under David Watson, St Michael-le-Belfrey was an ordinary Anglican parish. It represented the coming together of a particular person with his own outstanding gifts; a particular family with their own faith, vision and tensions; a particular moment in the life of the churches of a city and deanery and in the processes of English society in the seventies.

David Watson tried with incredible energy and undoubted success to create a fellowship in which a series of concentric circles of loving pastoral contact and responsibility would cover the whole of a growing congregation. Inevitably his own management style and abilities played a determinative role in the whole set-up. He developed a superb communication system, and sensitively nursed the Christian fellowship, and this side of their pastor was at least as important to the people of St Michael's as his preaching. There is to my mind, neither from Scripture or experience, any reason to be shy of the fact that a parish revolves around its minister. It may well be true therefore to say that if a parish wants renewal in the fashion of St Michael's it must, in addition to prayer and fasting, be prepared to empty itself and be led.

No one could conclude an assessment of this sort running the risk of leaving an impression that David was on some sort of ego-trip. Difficult though it was to combine his own personality with a systemic attempt at congregational organisation there is no doubt of the warmth, sincerity and attractiveness of that whole experience which became linked with his name. David suffered, I know, from our turning the microscope upon him and his work. It never was an easy thing to let yourself appear in public 'warts and all'. It is a small tribute to the size of the man that he welcomed and encouraged the exercise. Towards the end of his time at St Michael's there were being held twice a year church Renewal Weeks when upwards of a hundred and fifty visitors (clergy and lay leaders) came to York for seminars on what God was doing there and how he seemed to be leading them. There was never any attempt to hide the tensions and problems. Let one participant in such a week have the last word. 'Here we *felt* God's love in action. He was really among us. We go back believing he goes with us'.

Chapter Nine

SHARED LEADERSHIP

by

Graham Cray

Graham Cray joined the congregation of St Michael-le-Belfrey in 1975 when he became northern co-ordinator of the Church Pastoral Aid Society. He was appointed vicar of St Michael's in July 1978, during David Watson's time as rector.

David Watson 'phoned me on Wednesday 16th November, 1977. It was mid-evening, his day off and mine, so I was puzzled to receive his call. His secretary Judy was spending the evening with us so why not send a message? At the time I had been a member of the congregation of St Michael-le-Belfrey for just over two years, while fulfilling a travelling ministry as northern co-ordinator of the Youth Department of the Church Pastoral Aid Society (CPAS). David asked me what I was planning to do when my three-year appointment was up. Then he dropped his bombshell. Would I consider becoming vicar of St Michael's with him as rector—following the pattern pioneered by John Stott and Michael Baughen at All Souls Langham Place?

Over the next few weeks Jackie and I, the elders of St Michael's and the Archbishop of York all came to the conclusion that this appointment was what God wanted. On 16th December, one month after the original 'phone call, the Archbishop confirmed my appointment, which was to begin the following July. My most significant experience of David must be that, although I was only thirty years old and had never been a vicar, he trusted me with his church. It wasn't *his* church of course, and he never claimed that it was, just as it isn't mine now; but he trusted me to take over his role so that he would be free to travel full-time. During the four years of our vicar/rector partnership David never failed to support me, both privately and in public, and to trust me throughout a period which included many of the most painful events of our church's history.

David was a man of vision. He would say that Anne was the visionary, which was true in that she was often the first one to 'see' what God wanted for a particular aspect of the church's life. Many features of the ministry of St Cuthbert's and St Michael's came about through her prophetic gift and pastoral initiative. However, their gifts were complementary and equally necessary. If Anne was prophet and pastor, David was evangelist, teacher and the more overt leader of the whole work. David and Anne came to York in response to God's call and promise 'I will fill this house with my glory' (Haggai 2.7), but vision requires more than a call linked to a general promise. The leader with vision sees what the fulfilled promise could look like and leads the church towards it. Vision is practical as it sees the next step in the context of the future goal. Nor is it just a matter of goal-setting, but of revelation. David and Anne saw what God wanted St Cuthbert's and St Michael's, York to be. As they led the church to the next step, so their grasp of the ultimate goal continually broadened and deepened. This continual movement towards a deepening vision lies at the heart of biblical congregational growth for it is based on an interaction with the Word of God.

David and Anne invited me to become vicar because of their conviction that I shared their vision. In the autumn of 1977 I had gone to see Anne to talk about work with children. In my job with CPAS I was responsible for advising many parishes about their Sunday schools and I knew that Anne had pioneered a new approach in St Michael's 'Children's Workshop'. As we talked together, we realised that our vision and longing for the life of the local church was the same. This conversation proved to have been very significant when David and Anne began to look for a vicar for St Michael's. During the weekend of the 18th to the 20th of November, I attended St Michael's annual group leaders weekend at Lamplugh House at Thwing. During the Saturday afternoon, David, Anne and I walked through the local lanes and shared our understanding of God's vision for St Michael's, speaking both of what had already come into being and also of what we longed for, including the full participation of women in the overall leadership of the church. Later that afternoon we talked and prayed together in the Watsons' room. It was on the basis of common vision that David and Anne called Jackie and myself and on that basis that we accepted their call, having heard God's call in it.

David realised that the question of who would succeed him at York was a crucial one, for if the growth and realisation of vision is to continue beyond the first generation, it must be passed on. Paul's words to Timothy are of great importance: 'What you have heard from me before many witnesses, entrust to faithful men who will be able to teach others also' (2 Timothy 2.1). This presents a special problem in the Church of England. However much leadership has been shared, the appointment of a new incumbent is not finally in the hands of the congregation or of the existing lay leadership but of the patron—who may or may not be sympathetic to the more recent spiritual pilgrimage of a parish and who is in no way bound to consult the previous vicar.

On 1st October 1975, Jackie and I had moved to York to take up our ministry with CPAS. By then, many of the central features of the vision God had given David and Anne were already established. What struck us most was the quality of mutual love in the congregation, who for many years had been taught and shown that their love for one another was to be of the quality of Christ's love for them. We encountered a corporateness that quickly became a source of healing for both of us. Our first and lasting impression was not of David and Anne Watson and their gifts, but of the local expressions of the Body of Christ which had grown up under their ministry. We experienced the vision lived and fleshed out. Just as it is impossible to think of David's ministry apart from Anne's, so it became impossible for us to think of them in isolation from their fellow members of the fellowship of St Michael's.

The sense of corporateness was expressed in many ways: in area groups, a team of elders, an extended household in the rectory and in much talk of community. The other striking dimension of the church was the quality of the worship. The combination of expectancy through the shared experience of the presence of the Holy Spirit and of deeply committed relationships, released a freedom and richness in both the depth and variety of forms in worship. In January 1975 Andrew Maries had been appointed full time music director, supported by the rectory household. In July the Fisher-folk led a week's 'Festival of the Arts in Worship'. Both of these were formative events in bringing the vision for deeper worship, which David and Anne had received as far back as 1972, into the weekly experience of the congregation.

The next two years saw the vision take shape in ways that would become the hallmarks of David's later public ministry. At home in York a number of other extended households were formed, one to become the base for the

Mustard Seed café and shop. The first Renewal Week was held in order that the vision of renewal might be shared effectively with visitors who made special trips to York to ask advice and see what was happening. Riding Lights Theatre Company was formed. At the same time David's preaching ministry outside York was changing: instead of undertaking university evangelism and teaching on his own, he began to lead missions in cities and towns with a team of helpers. At first the Fisherfolk travelled with him; then, from February 1977, he began taking a team from St Michael's.

These were years of rapid growth and change; with hindsight perhaps some of the changes were too rapid. But in them the stage was being set for the 'home team' and the 'away team' of St Michael's ministry to work in parallel. At home we developed the vision and elsewhere we began to sow the seeds of it.

Our ministry 'away' was assisted by the publication of *I believe in Evangelism* in 1977 and *'I believe in the Church* in 1978.

Vision needs to be tested. Every congregation needs times when its vision and practice are examined by wise and experienced Christian leaders from outside its own ranks. It was with this intent that David invited John Poulton and a team representing ACE (the Archbishop's Council on Evangelism) to visit St Michael's between 17th and 23rd November 1977. As David has written in *You Are My God,* ACE suggested that a vicar/rector arrangement be established, and this confirmed what he and Anne had already begun to think. But ACE also came up with four matters which were to beome significant parts of the church's vision and agenda in the years that followed: the need to make radical changes in our area group network; to re-examine the full place of women in leadership; to examine the depth of our commitment to the kingdom of God in York, and the quality of our financial giving and stewardship. During the four years of my partnership with David, the first three of these items led to significant changes in the life and agenda of the church. The fourth item, concerning finance, caused a crisis as, for the first time, we struggled to pay our way—until we learned the pastoral lessons God was teaching us.

So David handed over the leadership of the church at a time when the agenda drawn up for us clearly implied that big changes were ahead. That was costly for him. He must have been tempted to hand over and yet try to keep control, but vision can never be the private possession of any individual or married couple, however gifted. The ultimate test of the leadership of anyone instrumental in the founding of a work of God is their ability to give it up to others so that it may continue to live and grow. I had wondered how fully David would trust me and release the 'home team' work to me, only to find that he did so completely in a comparatively short time, while always being supportive and trusting. The rightness of the decision and the depth of the letting go were to be tested very painfully in the next few years. Three major areas of costly learning and testing were related to vision and leadership.

The eldership had begun as a pastoral support to David in order that the work-load of ministry might be shared. Over the years the elders came to share more fully the overall authority and leadership of the church and David was able to be vulnerable and open with his fellow leaders. There was a considerable mutual submission amongst them, which David was part of. However there was also an inevitable dependance upon David. The eldership represented a reasonably successful compromise between two different structures: a corporate, interdependent leadership of peers, and a group of assistant leaders directed by one overall leader. By giving up the position of overall leadership, David made it possible for St Michael's to be led by a more interdependent corporate body. This still safeguarded the special legal role of the incumbent in the Church of England, but was a better embodiment of the vision. Since the congregation would inevitably model their vision upon it, shared leadership was crucial for the future development of St Michael's.

However, the team of elders was held together in part by common vision and in part by personal loyalty and commitment to David. When he stepped back the areas of disunity quickly surfaced. For about a year the elders struggled to reach a common mind, and the church, sensing what was happening, experienced a crisis of identity and direction. During much of this time David was away from York leading festivals with his team. When he returned he must sometimes have felt that he had let go of the helm only to see the ship founder on the rocks.

The long term result was to be the formation of an eldership of men and women with a greater unity and sense of corporateness than ever before. At the time that did not seem likely, and two major crises were to occur first.

Both the closure of the Mustard Seed shop and the painful split, resulting in a group leaving the congregation, are described in *You Are My God*. They were by far the most traumatic events in the life of our church and for that reason alone, I do not intend to re-open old wounds unnecessarily. Each of them contained a vital lesson about vision. The Mustard Seed eventually failed for a number of reasons, but the only one which is significant for our purposes is that when the project was

144

being set up, some of the elders were uneasy about it; not about the idea but about some of the specific plans. They so respected David's leadership that they never aired their doubts. Consequently the leadership of the church was never completely united behind the Mustard Seed shop. Tragically we only discovered this when a major crisis occurred, and then it was too late. The shop closed. I believe David had sensed that neither the elder-ship nor the congregation would mature into the full implication of the vision God had implanted within them until it stopped depending on him. This, as well as the need to free him for his ministry with the team, was the motivation behind his giving up his role with the congre-gation. Mercifully he could not have foreseen how trau-matic that necessary transition would prove.

The division which occurred was about vision. A group within the congregation found that the direction and emphasis which they believed the Holy Spirit was giving them was in conflict with the direction being taken by the church. This came to a head when I spoke about vision for the future in a series of sermons on leadership prior to the three-yearly appointment of elders. On the basis of those sermons, they considered that there was no longer a place for them in St Michael's and that they should withdraw as unobtrusively as possible. Like Abraham and Lot, they believed it was necessary to separate to find pasture without strife. Sadly it was quite impossible for that withdrawal to be unobtrusive; one was an elder, others group leaders; some had been in the fellowship for many years. Their leaving involved the most agonising tearing of relationships, and for David this was particularly painful. It came to a head when he was in Australia, having handed over his overall leader-ship. He was on the other side of the world and so his pain was increased by a sense of helplessness. The vision he held and had passed on to St Michael's focused on the unity of all believers in Christ as expressed in the local congregation, but this was a deep disagreement over vision. The choice seemed to be vision or unity.

When he returned, he publicly offered his support for the teaching that had been given, and he and I individually spent long hours with those who felt they had no choice but to leave, urging them to reconsider. As I look back now some form of parting of ways was inevitable. The two fellowships as they have emerged are so different in character and emphasis that it would have been almost impossible to hold together in one congregation such different understandings of leadership, family life, baptism etc. In particular St Michael's is committed to a pattern of renewal within the tradition of the Church of England—valuing that tradition as well as seeking its renewal. It was some of our more distinctively Anglican features that those who left found most difficult or irrelevant.

In the long term, the separation has freed both churches to grow with a fair degree of internal harmony. But at the time it was devastating and we were all at fault. We are now able to support and pray for one another both in public and private, even though we have to agree to differ on some matters, and some relationships are still tender. It may be that for David, the final healing of that hurt only came when he saw Jesus face to face and became like him.

The price of vision is pain, partly because our vision is always imperfect and incomplete. We do not yet *know* as fully as we are *known,* and the discovery of our blind spots is painful. We are also sinners and find a painful divide between our knowledge of God's will and our ability consistently to live it out. Added to this is the pain of other people's slowness or failure to respond. Sometimes it was only their sense of God's call which sustained David and Anne's vision—both at the beginning, when they were the only ones who had it, and later during painful crises or times of discouragement.

Without vision there can be no leadership. Without David and Anne's vision there would have been no St Cuthbert's and no St Michael-le-Belfrey—just two redundant church buildings. Vision has to become reality. To that end God equips his leaders in three ways: with a specific call, with specific gifts, and by making them examples—models of the vision lived out. David and Anne's call and gifts are obvious to anyone who hears the York story, but it was the example of their life, sometimes in weakness, pain and failure, which was the vital factor of their ministry; vision embodied in vulnerability.

David was painfully aware of and remarkably open about his weakness. His battles with bronchial asthma and deep depression are now well known. Both he and Anne have written very bravely about the struggles and stress in their marriage. In fact their standards of loving were so high, their love for one another so deep and their lives so open to hear the painful truth of what God still had to do in them, that it is no wonder that this was at times costly to their relationship. They have freely shared all this in conversations, talks, books and articles, and it is not for me to go beyond what they have already said. At times, like all of us, they would withdraw: but they would never pretend.

David's upbringing did not predispose him to vulnerability or make him a probable candidate for changing the face of the Church. From a military family, through public school, national service, Cambridge and ordination in the Church of England, his whole background encouraged him to 'keep himself to himself', with a 'stiff upper lip' to hide feelings and keep relationships polite but distant, and religion formal. Yet he learned to make radical changes in his life as his understanding of discipleship grew. He became vulnerable, committing himself deeply to his fellow Christians, sharing his inner self and his weaknesses, risking possible rejection, sharing his home and his leadership. None of us can or should be completely freed from the restrictions imposed by our background and David found some of these changes hard and painful, as well as joyous and liberating. He always remained a private, slightly formal man and beyond a certain depth it was easier to get to know Anne. But there was no question about the warmth of his welcome to the rectory when we got together to catch up with news whenever he returned from missions, nor about his painful honesty about himself.

His vulnerability was rooted in a ruthless determination to be open to God. He wanted to hear what God had to say, whoever it came through, and however it came. The youngest team member could 'speak the truth in love' to David, and a young clergyman be trusted as his successor. He knew that defensiveness and self-deception grieved and resisted the Spirit of truth and that the open confession of his weakness and need opened the door for the powerful grace of God. The depth of his ministry to others was rooted in this willingness to share his humanity and weakness and to trust the power of God. By his example he freed his audience to trust God for their own needs.

The tension between the demands of increasing time away from the love and the responsibilities of a family was particularly hard for both David and Anne, Fiona and Guy. Not only was there a conflicting demand on limited time, but there was also a painful question of identity. David found much of his sense of identity as a person in his work. He had an enormous capacity for work and drove himself very hard. Paradoxically, although his walk with God was deep and even intimate, and his willingness to obey his God total, for a long time he found it very hard simply to delight in being the loved child of a loving Father. It was not until the final year of his life that he was released from the necessity of work for identity. I do not wish to be misunderstood: it takes a man of very great stature to change so much and to be so vulnerable. Many Christians never approach the battleground which David entered because they do not have the courage to seek such costly grace or to become so vulnerable to God and to their brothers and sisters.

We shall not know in this life the *full* purposes of God in taking David from York such a short time before his illness and death, but two things are clear. The fellowship of St Michael-le-Belfrey has had to take full, mature and corporate responsibility under God for living out the expanding vision received through David and Anne; and God was able to do a deeper work of grace in his loved and vulnerable servant David.

Chapter Ten

THE AUTHOR

by

Edward England

Edward England was David Watson's publisher at Hodder and Stoughton from 1972 to 1980, and then for four years his literary agent and editorial adviser. He is Editor of *Renewal* magazine.

For twelve years I was privileged to be associated with David Watson's books but although we had a warm and indeed an affectionate relationship I sometimes felt that I knew him better through editing his manuscripts than through our meetings. Like others, I found him a private person. We met at his home in York and at my office in London; we had working lunches in a variety of hotels and restaurants, and made one or two short journeys together. We wrote each other scores if not hundreds of letters about the progress of a manuscript, a book jacket, a Swedish or German translation, getting books in quantity to Australia, New Zealand or Canada for a mission, and frequently concerning the nature of his future writing. Whether we met or wrote the agenda was normally so full that there was little time for personal sharing. Yet I can think of no author that I admired or loved more.

My first contact was in late 1972 when as a result of hearing one of his tapes on the Holy Spirit in a house group attached to Christ Church, Purley, in Surrey, I wrote on behalf of Hodder and Stoughton inviting him to write a book for us. I had known his name for several years through *Renewal* magazine which had published his articles and told of the dramatic growth at St Cuthbert's. I also knew him as the author of a Falcon publication *Towards Tomorrow's Church*. Hodders had a long tradition of publishing for Archbishops of York but I was to discover that bestsellers can come from a more humble address than Bishopsthorpe. To my surprise I received a complete book manuscript within a few days. I had expected to wait twelve months or so. No archbishop had ever matched that. *One in the Spirit* was a clear, concise and biblical account of the work of the Holy Spirit in the individual and the Church.

Hodders had pioneered in Britain the publishing of so-called charismatic books at a time when the traditional evangelical publishers were still maintaining that healings, tongues and prophecy, and some other gifts of the Spirit, were only for apostolic days. John Sherrill's *They Speak with other Tongues* and Michael Harper's *As at the Beginning* had actually been banned by some Christian bookshops. Michael Green's classic *I Believe in the Holy Spirit* had not yet been published.

I settled down to read *One in the Spirit* wondering into which camp it might fall. To my delight I saw that it was an attempt to unite Christians, to be a bridge between those who did not wish to see the gifts in operation in the Church and those who were in danger of abusing them. In his evangelistic missions in universities and churches David had witnessed how Christians divided over the work of the Spirit. 'My simple prayer in writing this book is that God may graciously use it, in a measure known only to him, to draw Christians together with a new desire to love one another as we love him, in obedience to Christ's command. I am not expecting for a moment that everyone will agree with what I have said.'

The content of *One in the Spirit* stemmed largely from the addresses he had given at the Annual Conference of the Colleges of Education Christian Unions, at Swanwick, in April 1972. Inter-Varsity Press, the publishing arm of the conference organisers, had expressed interest in publishing the addresses, and made some helpful comments on reading the initial manuscript. When its Publishing Committee saw the final manuscript however, its more conservative members, who did not share David's charismatic views, decided that the freedom he had been given in speaking should not be extended to his writing. In the one hundred pages of manuscript they recommended some fifty possible changes. Most were minor, a few crucial. David had deliberately aimed at some of the points of 'hot debate'. Unless adjustments were made the IVP could not proceed with publication. Several of David's friends confessed that they had compromised under similar pressure. He decided it would be a betrayal of what he believed.

The author was nursing his disappointment that publication was not to proceed when my letter arrived. I had no inside knowledge of the situation. His sense of rejection would have been lessened if he had known more of the publishing world. Every member of an IVP Publications Committee had been chosen as a trusted representative and guardian of traditional evangelical thought. Most would have appreciated the books of C. S. Lewis but if that celebrated author had submitted any manuscript to them it would have had to undergo the most rigorous editing. Even then I doubt if it would have made it.

Years later David looked back and saw that rejection as being in the providence of God. His books were going to bless a wider market than those of any British evangelical author. They were to be read by Protestants and Catholics, by high and low churchmen, and were to be translated into many languages. He needed the editorial freedom which a general publisher allowed to men of his stature and ability. Although all his manuscripts would be the subject of critical publishing reports before they went to the printer, he would be given complete freedom in the finalised script.

One in the Spirit was an immediate bestseller, going into reprint after reprint. When a writer in *Renewal* suggested that the IVP must be 'red in the face' regarding its success, their Publication Secretary, Ronald Inchley, who had built up a magnificent publishing programme from scratch, replied with feeling in a letter to the editor.

> This seems to suggest we gamble on the commercial success or failure of particular titles and that this is our main concern. Naturally we are pleased when, as in this case, the sale of a book is outstandingly good. But that is not our chief aim in publishing...The fact that David Watson's book, which began as a series of addresses at an IVF Conference, is selling so well does not surprise us in the least. For various reasons a particular book may suit one publishing house rather than another. The fact that there was no sense of rivalry nor anything disagreeable in the negotiations may be gauged perhaps from the generous acknowledgement of help received from IVP which David Watston included in his preface.

David was later to write *Live a New Life* for the IVP. He wanted it to be known there was no ill-feeling.

His first major book *I Believe in Evangelism* was published in 1976. The series editor, Michael Green, found that it enshrined principles of evangelism he had never seen in print before. 'It is rooted in experience. It is grounded in a remarkable grasp of the New Testament. It is alive with the freshness and power of the Holy Spirit. It will have a very great impact in inspiring congregational-based, worshipful evangelism in many parts of the world.'

David believed that with twice as many non-Christians in the world today as at the start of the century there was a greater urgency for evangelism than any other work. He was disturbed by the traditional pattern of Christians preaching only to Christians, failing to present Christ to the unconverted. He believed that preaching was the first and foremost means of making known God's word to God's world but his book made clear it was not the only means. It was the 'other means' that separated him from some of his more traditional brethren.

There were the signs and wonders which demonstrated the power of Christ. Healing was a means by which God spoke to an individual in order to communicate his love and the truth of the gospel. He told of an ex-professional boxer, with brain damage and partially paralysed, who had been instantly healed. The miracle had prepared his heart to receive the gospel.

He wrote that there was a place in evangelism for drama, dance, mime, painting, tapestry; all of which could tell of the glory of God and proclaim his handiwork. At times a silent presentation of God's truth could speak more loudly than words.

In an age dominated by television, glossy magazines and the popular daily newspapers he saw the need to present God visually as well as audibly. He quoted David in Psalm 19 speaking of God's revelation both in his creation and in his word; 'The heavens are *telling* the glory of God; and the firmament *proclaims* his handiwork; Day to day pours forth *speech,* and night to night *declares* knowledge.'

An elderly Christian couple whom I love dearly invited me to Sunday tea fearing I was in danger of sponsoring an 'unsound' author. Graciously but firmly they questioned me about David. Dance, drama, mime as methods of evangelism? Hadn't I read Martyn Lloyd-Jones'

Preaching and Preachers? Yes, I told them, I had published it. And didn't David Watson advocate a social gospel? A bit, I confessed. From my reading of his work I had found that like Jesus he believed we should care for the bodies and minds of men as well as for their spiritual condition. 'Evangelism is making disciples of all nations, and loving our neighbour as ourselves.' They wrote to David at some length but if they did receive a reply it had not changed their views when next I met them.

I agreed to Michael Green's suggestion that David be invited to write a second volume in the *I Believe* series, this time on *The Church.* It was the most difficult book he was to write. The problem was where to start or stop on a subject so vast. The more he worked on the revisions of the original manuscript the more clearly he saw the glaring omissions, scanty references to huge themes, and what he described as his personal ignorance on some of the crucial issues of the day.

If *I Believe in the Church,* published in 1978, was not a major theological treatise, it was rightly described by Michael Green as that much rarer contribution to the Christian reading public: a thoughtful, intelligent and above all 'earthed' presentation of what, according to the Bible, God intends his Church to be like.

Double the length of an average novel, more than three times as long as *One in the Spirit,* it was a remarkable achievement for a busy clergyman, with a crowded church, who was also involved in missions and festivals. Those outside engagements and the time he gave to writing threatened his pastoral work at times and led him to search his heart and the Scriptures to discover the principles of shared leadership within the body of Christ. When he wrote of the vicar becoming a bottle-neck he was drawing on personal experience.

The vicar or minister is usually the bottle-neck, if not the cork, of his church; nothing can go in or out except through him. No meetings can be made without his counsel and approval. I know of some parishes where the laity cannot even meet for Bible study or prayer unless the vicar is present. This bottle concept of ministry makes growth and maturity virtually impossible. Members are unable to develop into the God-given ministry they could well experience because, in structure and in practice, there is room for only one minister. It is no doubt because of this that the fire of the Spirit has resulted in the bottle exploding into numerous house fellowships or house churches where there is room for growth and for the sharing of ministry. Unless there are new wine-skins for the new wine, some bursting out is inevitable.

The book was a trifle untidy and did not answer satisfactorily all the issues it raised but it had special value because it came out of day-to-day experience in a developing parish. He confessed that the church in York did not yet embody all the ideas he proposed. He was still puzzling over the ordination of women, indeed on the whole question of ministry. He quoted Michael Harper's statement: 'To ordain women will only add to the confusion: it will simply perpetuate the caste system, only include women as well as men. We shall be no better off.' He appeared to have some sympathy for the provocative remark of a theological college tutor: 'The problem is not when we can start ordaining women, but when we can stop ordaining men.' He vexed some readers by his statement: '*In general* (always dangerous!) women *may* not be able to grasp and hold firmly the delicate balance of Christian *doctrine* as well as men. By the very intuitiveness of their nature, women may see certain issues much more quickly and clearly than men—and by the same impulse be more strongly tempted off on a tangent and away from the biblical balance of the "whole counsel of God."' He was in greater trouble, especially in Wales and Northern Ireland, over the views he expressed on the unity of the Church. He did not want to ignore the lessons of history in a search for reunion but believed that we should not be trapped by the past.

> What helpful contribution to the tragic situation in Ulster today is the annual celebration (for the Protestants) of the Battle of the Boyne in 1690?...Although some of the reasons for our divisions may be defensible—though probably nothing like so defensible as we may think—our *attitudes* towards others as we maintain and perpetuate those divisions are nearly always inexcusable. Christian groups and churches are notoriously negative and suspicious towards one another, fearing the worst instead of believing the best.

Between the thirties and the mid sixties Dr Leslie Weatherhead had been Hodders best-selling Christian author. It gave me great joy to introduce as his successor into that top position a man like David whose authority was the word of God. Weatherhead had retired by the time I arrived at Hodders in 1966 but I found that those to whom his views are unacceptable could sometimes benefit from a study of his style. I sent David a copy of *How can I find God?* which Hodders had reprinted constantly from the 1930s to the early 1970s. It asked three simple questions: Do I really want to find God?; Where can I find God?; What will happen if I find God? I asked David to write a similar evangelical book for today. *Is Anyone There?* was published in 1979. It was for those who at one moment want to find God, and at the next are anxious to flee from him. It owed nothing to Weatherhead's theology but the inspiration and not a few of the ideas came from that earlier volume.

I ventured after long discussion that his next book

should be on discipleship. I did not know whether to feel pleased or guilty when he wrote: 'Every time I write a book I wonder really why I am doing it, but you have given me the motivation to try again!' *Discipleship* was produced during an exceptionally busy year. His letters told of exhausting missions, tours which were too long, from which he returned very tired, having battled with bugs, sleepless nights and lots of changes. And later:

> I am trying hard to complete the manuscript on *Discipleship*, but still have about three chapters to go, and I have a massive teaching schedule at Fuller and Regent College in January for which I must prepare soon. Therefore I doubt if it will be available until the end of February, but I shall try to complete it by then if at all possible.

Hard-pressed as he was, the next paragraph went on to ask if I would like a modern version of *Pilgrim's Progress*.

> There are so many slurs and tangents which take the Christian off the main path, that it might be worth trying to set this in allegorical form, rather than done in a straight doctrinal book. It might be too difficult to do, and of course it would be impossible to reproduce anything of the magnificence of *Pilgrim's Progress*. However, I wondered if this sort of idea appealed to you as a possibility for the future.

I wasn't sure, but responded positively to an approach from a journalist on the *Sunday Express* who thought David might write a regular column. David was about to go overseas but suggested 'I could send the articles from Australia rather than letting them go cold on it.' The evangelist in him was always seeking to get beyond the church, outside the Christian bookshop. Specimen articles were written but the series never materialised.

Others may know whether his work-load contributed

to his depression or was a partial escape from it. Several of our most creative writers, secular and religious, suffered similarly. I shared with him how Dr J. B. Phillips, whose translation of the New Testament had made him into an international figure, knew similar and even greater periods of darkness. Phillips would telephone to describe the mental pain which in his case seemed beyond the reach of any medication.

David described the crushing burden of physical and mental tiredness. 'Even after a simple evangelistic service, the effort of preaching Christ and seeking to convince men about him, has frequently left me drained and exhausted. I can think of few activities that are more demanding.' He knew that depression is not necessarily a sign of spiritual failure. Some of the greatest saints have suffered from it. But depression could sometimes have a spiritual cause. In his depression God came to David with words similar to those he spoke to Elijah: 'I know you're depressed because there hasn't been a revival in spite of all that has happened. I know you want me to come down in a dramatic way on my people, but I'm not doing so. However, I'm in control, I haven't forsaken you, I love you still, and I am working, as I often do, so secretly and silently that you hardly notice it.'

A writer reveals more of himself than he intends. In David's books when he mentions suffering he usually includes depression. Elijah's experience was obviously a comfort to him. 'God did not send Elijah spiritual counsel or rebuke his pride, rebellion and self-pity, but sent him long refreshing periods of sleep, two nourishing meals and six weeks of complete rest and change!...Many Christians today are depressed partly or wholly from sheer physical exhaustion.'

On my fiftieth birthday I confided that I had told Hodders I was going to leave in three months, convinced that my work was to take a fresh direction. 'Is there any chance that you might reconsider your decision?' he replied. 'Your position at Hodders is strategic.' At his prompting another Christian leader wrote similarly. When I created a literary agency to look after Christian authors, not only for Hodders but for a variety of Christian publishers, David became my first author.

He would often quote the advice which Richard Foster gives in *Celebration of Discipline*: 'Develop a habit of giving things away. If you find that you are becoming attached to some possession consider giving it to someone who needs it.' On several occasions I endeavoured to persuade David not to give away so readily the copyright, and therefore the income, from his books to a charitable trust. I wanted him and his family to enjoy some personal benefit from the hard work and success but he seemed set not to benefit financially from his writing. He knew of the lifestyle of some American evangelists who run weekly television shows and was happier living at the level of the average Church of England clergyman. He liked the simplicity which Foster described as 'the singleness of purpose which liberates us from the passion to accumulate and possess.'

Lion published *Jesus: Then and Now,* an illustrated volume of which David was joint-author, in 1982. It was based on material from the videos which he had made with Trinity Trust. Hodders were keen to publish the book and I wanted them to do so, but it was an occasion on which I advised him wrongly. It finished up with Lion Publishers and because of their expertise with illustrated colour books, they produced a better and more competitively priced volume than Hodders would have done.

The same autumn Hodders published his volume of daily devotional readings *Through the Year with David Watson,* edited by Jean Watson (no relation) who had taken the material from his many tapes, letters, sermon notes and books. Like many of his books it was published in America by Harold Shaw Publishers, but the title there was *Grow and Flourish*.

I will always remember Christmas 1982. On Christmas Eve, with the last of the greeting cards and the turkey, the typescript of his autobiography *You Are My God* arrived. Because he wanted a response before his proposed visit to America early in the New Year I started reading it on Christmas morning, with my family's permission! For years David had resisted the pressure to write about York, believing 'the growth of a congregation from almost nothing to seven hundred or more can be overrated.' Both at St Cuthbert's and St Michael-le-Belfrey they had suffered from too much exposure. Added to that, he knew that the apparent triumphalism of Christian success stories could sometimes discourage those who were battling with ordinary problems. He was also aware of the spiritual dangers of the 'cult of the personality'. 'This is acceptable in the secular sphere of superstars, but it is divisive in the Christian church.'

He needed reassurance from me, not only a rapid come-back. A valued friend who had seen part of the manuscript during its preparation, a clergyman for whom David had the highest esteem, had advised him to wait ten years before publishing. 'He wants me to put it on ice,' David wrote to me. 'Obviously, I cannot do this—for many reasons—and I hope the book will be useful. I sense he is afraid of my sharing some of the weaknesses and problems, etc. Nevertheless, I am reading what I have written very critically.'

I saw at once why his friend, concerned only for David, wanted him to put the manuscript into cold storage. It had a degree of openness and honesty not normally found in Christian autobiography. Christian leaders proclaimed and wrote about the strengths and weakness of Bible characters—of Moses, David and the apostle Peter—but were less frank, and probably with good reason, when telling their own story. Honesty in autobiography is terribly hard to achieve and afterwards can be difficult to live with.

'No human frailty,' David wrote, 'need be a hindrance to God's infinite grace...My ultimate purpose is to give a personal testimony to the reality of God in the varied spectrum of human experience. If through the sunshine and storms something of the light of Christ is seen in greater glory, this book will not be in vain.'

He had written as frankly about home life as about the church. 'Both Anne and I know that Christians have no immunity from the marriage problems that afflict society so widely today. For this reason we agreed that I should be open about the difficulties that we too have experienced, especially now that we have worked through these traumas to a more mature and strong relationship.' I recommended a few minor cuts, a sentence here, a word there, and some changes in the final pages, but as both David and Anne were courageous enough to share I saw no reason for delaying publication. Anne had given wise counsel during the writing of the manuscript and supported David in his decision to proceed with publication.

That Christmas I was haunted by the way that suffering and blessing seemed inseparable. Some years before I had written that great books came out of great suffering, and illustrated this with titles like the *Pilgrim's Progress*, *The Hiding Place* and *Joni*, but now I saw that a powerful ministry often had the same roots. I mentioned this to David. Within days, on 5th January 1983, I had a telephone call to say that he was in hospital. Cancer of the colon was suspected.

'No!' I cried. 'Not cancer. Hasn't he suffered enough already?'

I did not know that this year of 1983 was to be the year when, through radio, television, videos and books, he would reach more men than ever for Christ.

I joined earnestly with the thousands who prayed for his recovery following the operation. A letter came from David at the end of January. He had cancelled everything until Easter. 'But from Easter I could perhaps do some useful writing. Any thoughts—in due time—would be appreciated.' I suggested he kept a journal. (I had been with my wife on a weekend course on keeping a journal for personal growth.) His response was prompt. 'I'll try to keep a journal as soon as I feel strong enough to write/dictate. I'm sure it could be valuable—perhaps a *small* book written by Anne and me sometime? (Reactions to cancer—feelings, fears, faith.)'

In mid March we sat in his study and discussed some book topics. We limited our time together to thirty or forty minutes as he was still not strong. I spent two-thirds of the time outlining the volume which I hoped he would write on forgiveness. It would be a companion volume to *Discipleship*, and include every aspect of the subject from the forgiveness which God offers to us in Christ to forgiveness within the family and community. It had been a constant theme in his preaching. Indeed one of his favourite stories concerned his friend Bishop Festo Kivengere who had an argument with his wife one evening. Afterwards he had to go out and preach, so he said goodbye but as he walked down the drive God spoke to him.

'Festo,' said the Lord, 'you go back and apologise to your wife.'
'But Lord, I've got a very important sermon to preach.'

'You go and apologise to your wife.'

'But Lord, there are hundreds of people waiting for me and we're going to have a good time tonight.'

'You must go and apologise to your wife.'

'But Lord, I'm almost late and someone's waiting to collect me.'

'All right,' the Lord said, 'you go and preach your sermon and I'm going to stay with your wife in the kitchen.'

Bishop Festo went back into the kitchen and apologised. 'So there was revival in the kitchen before there was revival in the church,' the Bishop said afterwards.

David quoted the superintendent of a mental hospital who said he would be able to send a large percentage of his patients home cured if only they could be assured of forgiveness. As my time with him was drawing to a close David turned to me and asked me if *Forgiveness* was really the book I wanted him to write. I hesitated.

'I'm almost frightened to suggest it, David,' I said, 'but what I'd really like, if it isn't too painful, is a book about cancer. I'd like you to share your present experiences. A book like that would be read by non-Christians far more than a devotional title.'

I had been hesitant about mentioning the topic because I wasn't sure of my motivation in doing so and I shared this with David. Publishers like bestsellers. A lack of sensitivity, or awareness of what God wanted David to do, might result in my encouraging unwisely. My wife, a doctor, had mentioned to me before leaving home that it might be beneficial if he did not dwell on his illness. I told David this. I also recalled how Brian Hession, an Anglican minister who had cancer in the 1950s, had penetrated the secular book market with *Determined to Live*.

'Please don't say yes now,' I said. 'Talk it over with Anne, and the folk in the Belfrey Trust. I'm not sure that I know the mind of God in this.'

I sent him *Determined to Live*. A few days later he wrote: 'I would like to have a go at my personal story of facing cancer and death. I certainly hope to be more realistic about the future than perhaps Brian Hession was in his own book. I would still like to keep the possibility of a later book on forgiveness.'

He thought of something short, about ninety-six pages. I recommended a minimum of one hundred and sixty pages if it was going to hit the general bookshops. It must start dramatically: with his visit to the doctor a few days after Christmas with the news that hit him like a thunderbolt. 'It can't be true. That sort of thing doesn't happen to me.'

His faith that God healed today would be a powerful ingredient. He had seen many healed in answer to prayer and he believed that God could heal him. The book would clarify that faith but include a clear recognition of the sovereignty of God. It would examine the mystery of why some are healed and others are not. I did not like his two title suggestions: *From Cancer to Life* or *Learning to live with Cancer*; I wanted to keep the emotive word in a sub-title. I responded positively to *Fear No Evil*.

As he started to write what was to be his final book, I found myself turning again to see what he had written on healing. He was convinced that healing was, and still is, very much a part of the church's mission. 'Simplistic teaching about healing must, of course, be rejected,' he wrote in 1978. 'It is not true that "if you have faith, you will be healed"; and such a suggestion can have disastrous consequences, leading to deep depression, feelings of failure, and perhaps utter despair.'

'I do not know why some are healed when prayed for and some are not,' he wrote in 1982. 'I do not know why four young people with cancer, three of them parents, all died within months, when as a congregation in York we had prayed and fasted for them as we had never done before. But I do know that if I could understand all God's ways he would be no bigger than my mind and not worth believing in. I do know that the primary question to ask is not "why" but "what"—"Lord, what are you saying in this?"'

He was especially helpful on the fact that in all healing God is sovereign. First, in his *timing*. 'Why was the cripple from birth laid daily at the Gate Beautiful, until the time at last came for him to be healed, as recorded in Acts 3?'

Secondly, in the *conditions*. 'Various books on healing suggest reasons some people are not healed in answer to prayer: lack of repentance, lack of faith, lack of commitment to Christ, etc. But in the Gospels there were often no conditions attached at all. With many, there was no sign of repentance or faith; they were not yet disciples of Christ; in other words there was no spiritual reason why they should have been healed, apart from the matter of God's sovereignty.'

Thirdly, he saw that God was sovereign in *limiting* his power. He pointed out that the centurion's servant was healed with only a 'word' and at a distance. 'But why did he not say the word for countless others all over Palestine, let alone the rest of the world?'

Fourthly, God was sovereign *in the nature of the sickness he healed*. 'While we are told sometimes that he healed every disease, it seems that he was usually concerned with those diseases which were beyond the power of physicians to heal, for one reason or another, such as the woman with haemorrhage.... A clear recognition of the sovereignty of God, even in the healing ministry of God, may help us in what is an extraordinary puzzling aspect of the church's total mission.'

In April there was an overwhelming response to his

BBC broadcast on Radio 4 with Nick Page. In May there was a fresh call for prayer. A medical scan had revealed that the tumour had grown considerably, although his general condition was good. A general feeling of well-being enabled him to begin some active ministry, thankful for what he described as the 'sabbatical' he had enjoyed with his family. In June he was strong enough to go to the Lake District to speak to the Hodder salesmen at their summer conference. He talked little about his books and a lot about Christ. It was said there had probably never been a more powerful author-appearance at a sales conference.

In mid September he asked me to call and collect all but the last two chapters of *Fear No Evil*. Knowing the demands there had been that summer for preaching, radio talks, and newspaper interviews, I found it difficult to guess how he had made the time to write the eighteen chapters he gave me.

I opened the manuscript on the train journey from Charing Cross station to Tunbridge Wells but before the train had reached London Bridge my heart sank. He had written the wrong book! A worthy treatise on suffering. There were fragments of experience sandwiched between reflections on pain and death, and long quotations from authors who expressed themselves with less lucidity than David did himself. His keen mind was thinking it all out, facing the unanswerable questions with his intellect, but there was too little about himself, his emotions. I should have known. David the persuasive evangelist, the outstanding communicator, shared the Gospel more easily than he shared himself. I had wanted his story: he had given us his argument. It was head not heart material. The book must have both. I had failed him by not asking to see thirty or so pages in May. Had I done so this situation would have been avoided. Here was one of

Christendom's finest communicators not communicating.
I endeavour to respond to all manuscripts within forty-
eight hours. I did so on this occasion, warmly congratu-
lating him on the achievement of writing the book ahead
of schedule and promising to write again in a day or two
with a detailed response.

My first thought was to put a narrative writer alongside
him. My wife pointed out however that he was himself a
more able person than anyone I could find at short
notice. She urged me to give him an honest reaction,
going through the manuscript page by page, and to pray
that he would have the courage and strength to respond.
The sermons, the preaching, the weary quotations, must
go. We needed a book that would be intellectually satis-
fying, that would face the hard questions, but all within
the content of his own experience taking us week by
week through 1983. He needed to recall the conversations, as best he could, at critical moments. What had
Anne said to him, what had she done when she heard
that he had cancer? How had they told the children? We
needed to go to the operating theatre with him, to hear
the verdict of the surgeon after the operation when he
was asked: 'How long have I got?' and to react ourselves
to the reply, 'We can't really say. Perhaps a year. Maybe
more, maybe less.' We would listen to the things God
was saying to him, we would accept his spiritual insights,
his biblical exposition *if* we sat where he sat.

A measure of David Watson's greatness was his response. He pencilled out days in his diary in October and
early November to rework the book before sending it to
other advisers. Thankfully, he had the use of a word
processor, the help of a magnificent secretary, Hilary
Saunders, and the wise counsel of Anne.

Six weeks before Christmas the postman delivered the
new manuscript. I wept as I read it. *Fear No Evil* was

everything that I had hoped for. Apart from some tidying up in three chapters there was nothing to be changed.

'I do not think,' I wrote to him, 'I have ever read a manuscript which moved my heart more deeply. It is a book that I wish with all my heart you had never had the opportunity of writing, but in the situation in which you find yourself I am so thankful to God you have set time aside to put it all down on paper. It is not a story of cancer but of God being with you when passing through the waters.'

In early January, at proof stage, he wrote a four-page epilogue: 'Whatever else is happening to me physically, God is working deeply in my life… In that position of security I have experienced once again his perfect love, a love that casts out all fear.'

Our last meeting was almost a year after his operation, in the study of his London home. I stayed only forty-five minutes. He had been taking large doses of steroids for his asthma. Because his legs and ankles were swollen he sat in a low chair with his feet propped up at a slightly higher level. His abdomen was swollen. 'I feel a bit as if I'm pregnant,' he laughed, pouring himself some iced water from a flask. Physically he was feeble but his mind was clear as ever, his faith rock-like.

Hodders had fixed the publication date for *Fear No Evil* in May. 'I may not be around on publication day,' he said. I said nothing. He had sometimes told the story of how when F. B. Meyer was dying, he sent a last postcard to his great friend Lindsay Glegg. In shaky handwriting he wrote, 'I have raced you to heaven. I am just off. See you there. Love, F. B. Meyer.'

He was not afraid of death. He said he had been meditating on Philippians 1. 'For me to live is Christ, and to die is gain. But if I live on in the flesh, this will mean fruit from my labour, but what I shall choose I cannot tell. For I am hard pressed between the two, having a desire to depart and be with Christ, which is far better.'

His great friend, John Collins of Holy Trinity, Brompton, who had been instrumental in leading him to Christ at Cambridge, had suggested that God might have two plans: Plan A and Plan B. In Plan A God was saying, 'Come home, David. Your work is finished.' In Plan B, 'Can you endure a little more, a little longer? There is more work to be done.' 'I found that helpful,' David said. He looked at his swollen abdomen. 'I feel my ministry is not finished, whatever the evidence to the contrary.'

Of course, he was right. His ministry was not finished. More copies of his books have been sold in the year since his death than in the previous five years. And they will go on ministering to readers not only in English but in German, Swedish, Finnish, Afrikaans, Chinese and other languages.

Chapter Eleven

THE FRIEND

by

Sylvia Mary Alison

Sylvia Mary Alison is Chairman of the Prison Fellowship in England and Wales and, as wife of Michael Alison MP, is a member of the Parliamentary Wives' Christian Fellowship. A close friend of the family and god-mother to Fiona Watson, she has known the Watsons since 1965.

I first met David in 1965. The daughter of friends of ours in Yorkshire was ill and a little group of us had been praying for her. At the suggestion of David MacInnes, I got in touch with David Watson, who had just been appointed curate of St Cuthbert's at York, so that we might go and pray with her together. David and Anne met me at York station. We went together to Rosie's room in hospital, and as we prayed with her her stomach, greatly distended by a mysterious illness, went down two inches. By the end of that week she was able to go home. Although she died of cancer a few years later, she experienced a remarkable remission for some time.

From that time onwards a deep friendship grew up between the three of us. In those early days David, Anne and I often met to pray for the congregation of St Cuthbert's, and we went parish visiting together as a three-some. This went on until their daughter Fiona (my god-daughter) was born, after which time Anne was of necessity housebound. By then the congregation was growing and David had other helpers.

Michael and I used to take our children to the family service at St Cuthbert's which at first had a small congregation. Soon it grew to need two family services, then before long we had to arrive early if we didn't want to be in the extension—a hall not far away into which the service was relayed.

We regarded David and Anne as family; they had the key to our house, which they used for their days off while we were in London, and they often came over for the day while we were at home. This went on for some years until a friend lent them a cottage of their own, to which they could retreat with their growing children in complete privacy.

Anne was a shy and diffident girl when I first met her. I remember on one occasion knocking on the Rectory door and when Anne came to open it she looked at me nervously: 'David is not in,' she said. 'But that doesn't matter,' I replied, 'I haven't come to see David, I've come to see you!' Surprised, she led me into the sitting-room and we started to talk. I soon realised that she felt an outsider: that nobody was interested in her, that they only wanted to see David and that she was irrelevant. As the wife of a Member of Parliament, I could understand how she felt. I think it was a feeling which remained with Anne for many years.

David has talked in his autobiography of tensions in their marriage and I see these as nothing out of the ordinary. They lived in a hothouse, constantly in the public eye, and the pressures on them both were very great. They came from different backgrounds and had different expectations of what a husband or wife should be, of what parents should be like, of what the role of a clergyman's wife should be. This is nothing unusual and something that every couple has to come to terms with, but because increasingly they lived their lives communally, particularly after their move to St Michael-le-Belfrey, any tensions between them became public property. They worked courageously and hard at the relationship. They had a deep love and an enormous respect for each other, and the work in York was able to grow because of the variety of gifts which they jointly held. By the time they came to London in the autumn of 1982 they had come to a new depth of relationship. It was tragic that they had so little time together, but wonderful that Anne as a nurse was able to care for David during his last illness. Had they had a second twenty-year period of life together, I am sure they would have developed into a remarkable husband and wife team.

I hold it a great honour and privilege to have had David and Anne as friends; it has been rare in my experience to have equally as friends both a man and his wife. When they moved to London David wrote and asked me to be a trustee of the Belfrey Trust; to be one of those friends with whom he could think and pray through his life and ministry. I was thrilled that they were coming to London because we would be able to see more of them all.

That November, whilst he was in Canada with his team, David rang me because he was concerned about Anne in their new home in London, as she was deeply depressed by another of his long absences. He asked me to go and see her and find out how she really was, and if I thought he should come home then he would fly straight back to be with her. I talked to Anne and between us we decided that she could cope and that it would be best for David to complete his Canadian programme; but we resolved to try and persuade him and his organisers to make future trips away from home less long. I rang him in Canada and told him this, so he stayed until the end of the programme. I felt so honoured and humbled that he should accept my decision and act accordingly.

At Christmas he gave Michael and me the manuscript of his autobiography *You Are My God* to read, asking us for our comments. In exchange I gave him the first few chapters of the book I had begun to write, *God is Building a House*, and asked for his comments. We had already returned his manuscript and made our appreciative remarks when he telephoned on the morning of Friday, 7th January 1983. He was due to fly to California on the Monday, with his team, to lead seminars at Fuller Theological Seminary. 'I am ringing you to make some comments on your book' he said, 'but before I do that, I should tell you that I've seen a specialist this morning and I have got to go into hospital for a serious abdominal operation on Monday.' I was stunned. It was totally unexpected. We went on to discuss his illness, and he told me it was cancer. Then he said, 'Now let's talk about your book!' I protested feebly, in a complete daze and knowing how unimportant my book was in comparison with his news. But he solemnly went through the various points as if he had nothing else on his mind at all.

On 9th January he returned my manuscript with a letter, which ends: 'I'm sorry this is so scrappy. There's a lot to do before I go into Guy's Hospital tomorrow morning! Keep an eye on Fiona and Guy and Anne if you will. They will be under extra pressure in the next few weeks...' During the last year of David's life I learnt a lot about friendship and love. How easy it is to take friends for granted, and never to let them know how much we appreciate them until it is too late.

David had his operation on a Thursday. On the Friday morning Anne and I went to the hospital together. David's surgeon told Anne that although the operation had gone well, secondaries had developed in the liver. She asked him how long he had to live. 'About a year,' he said. We sat in the passage and wept. The Chaplain kindly took us into a side room and made us tea and after a while, Anne went to be with David. Later she emerged from the ward and said that he would like to see me too. I sat beside him and held his hand. He had tubes all around his face. There wasn't much to say. When he commented that no one had mentioned how long he was likely to live, I told him what I had heard the surgeon say, 'About a year, I think; but do ask him yourself.'

For a few months David grew stronger. As he was told he should not work before Easter, he was for once able to spend time relaxing with Anne. In the summer he started work again and came and led several Bible readings with the Parliamentary Wives' Christian Fellowship. In the autumn he was much better and embarked on a huge programme of engagements. However, the tumour on his liver had not decreased in size: it was growing. He has written his own story of those last days in *Fear No Evil*. Those of us who knew him and were with him and met at trustees meetings to discuss his programme were deeply moved and impressed by his enormous courage, sense of humour and complete assurance that God is sovereign and trustworthy, in spite of all the apparent setbacks. David and Anne came to supper with us in October, and they insisted on praying for Michael and me rather than us for them. In January I had lunch with them both and Fiona, and David was laughing about his thin arms and legs–'a matchstick man'.

We went to his last sermon preached at St Michael's, Chester Square, in mid January. He had to sit on a stool to preach, but spoke movingly and humorously, totally without self-pity or self-dramatisation. The next day he took a turn for the worse, and thereafter became increasingly weaker. I last saw him late in January, just before I went to the United States for a week. Anne and Fiona called me into his room, where he had just woken from sleep. He was happy to have his wife and daughter there, and was looking forward to Guy's return from school. He was very thin and very weak. I gave him a kiss and said goodbye. It felt very final.

Three months after his death the Parliamentary Wives' Group gave Anne a week's package tour in Venice as a love-gift. I accompanied her, and we spent a marvellous time together, talking, laughing, crying, and exploring the marvels of Venice. Poor Anne had had a very traumatic time, nursing her dying husband, then facing his death and funeral and the remarkable Memorial Services in York Minster and St Paul's Cathedral. She had sent out personally one hundred copies of his book *Fear No Evil* before publication, which was to be the day after we returned from Venice. She was very tired and far from well herself, yet I was again struck by her wonderful insight and understanding and by the closeness of her walk with the Lord. What a very fine partner she was for David.

David and Anne were pioneers; their ministry broke new ground by bringing together Christians of all denominations and by introducing new forms of worship through dance, drama, mime and music. The end of David's life has not brought this ministry to an end, and the Belfrey Trust continues with Anne as Director. We have yet to see what God will do through her and through the many people who have glimpsed a new vision as a result of David's work.

Chapter Twelve

THE FINAL YEARS

by

Teddy Saunders

The Reverend Teddy Saunders has been Chairman of the Belfrey Trust, which was formed to advise and support the ministry of David Watson. He was until recently the Rector of St Michael's, Chester Square, London.

I don't remember having met David Watson before 1980, except very briefly when he was a curate in Cambridge and once at a conference in 1978 when I doubt if we did more than exchange greetings. But in May 1980 the Chelsea Council of Churches sponsored a festival called 'To London with Love' which was led by David, and I was particularly delighted to be invited to join in. Later that week my wife Margaret, feeling deeply grateful for David's ministry and making an inspired guess at what his absence must cost Anne, whom neither of us had ever met, wrote her a special letter with a small love-gift. A friendship had begun.

We had no idea how much David and Anne needed friendship, even at that time, but especially during the next few years. We had no idea how deeply involved we were to become in their lives, and how grievously we were to suffer with them through David's terminal illness. Indeed we had no thoughts of getting involved with them beyond normal Christian fellowship and practical help should this be needed.

I think it was at some stage in 1980 that the question was first raised of the Watsons leaving York and moving to London, but it did not make any progress until later that year when John Collins had become vicar of Holy Trinity Brompton in South Kensington. David talked of moving to London partly because he felt his ministry in York had finished and partly because London might well be a strategically significant centre from which to travel and in which to live. When it seemed right to explore it further David asked for the advice of the Archbishop of York, Stuart Blanch, who warmly approved. Eventually the decision was made.

Suddenly I found myself trying to plan with David and John just how to set up a new structure to facilitate the move and to enable David's ministry to be exercised most effectively afterwards. David was a minister of the Church of England and that ancient institution makes no provision for ministry except in a parish or on the staff of a diocese. David would therefore need the Bishop of London's licence (which was enthusiastically granted), a house in which to live, a fund to support him and his work, a local church where he and his family could worship and support could be obtained, and staff to help him both administratively and ministerially.

David and John discussed the obvious solution that he should be 'attached' to Holy Trinity Brompton as an extra and honorary member of their staff, and after a period of prayerful negotiation with the leaders of the church this was agreed. When he came to London it was clearly understood that he came to join HTB and to have some share in the ministry.

David's travelling and missionary work had been supported for some time by a specially established charitable trust, and it was proposed that this be used to fund his future work with an enlarged trusteeship. He asked me to become one of the new trustees and eventually this invitation was extended to becoming chairman. John was also to be a trustee, as were Sylvia Mary Alison,

Michael Warren, and Douglas Greenfield who had worked so closely and loyally with David from York and who was to continue to do so quite invaluably. Crispin Joynson-Hicks (now Lord Brentford), Ian Anderson and Peter Collier continued as trustees. We called it the 'Belfrey Trust' to mark its origins.

The question of a home for the Watson family was more difficult. Eventually the Trust was offered a house which the Grosvenor Estate had been hoping to sell but were willing to withdraw from the market and let us have for the Watsons at a reasonable rent. David and Anne were delighted with it, though it was a bit further from HTB than we wanted. An excellent mews house with a garage and a small garden not far from Eaton Square, it was exactly what we needed for the family, and there was just enough room for a secretary to work until funds for an office and HQ elsewhere could be found.

David and Anne did not feel confident about sharing their limited home space with an unknown London secretary however competent, so it seemed that a temporary solution was needed. My daughter Hilary was just completing a year working for Dick Lucas at St Andrew's Undershaft after finishing her degree at Durham University. By no stretch of the imagination did her experience qualify her to be considered a competent secretary, but David wondered whether while they were settling into London and the work-load was beginning to build up, Hilary might be a 'temporary solution'. She astonished us all by becoming absolutely invaluable to David, a real support and encouragement to Anne, and an older sister and friend to Fiona and Guy.

From York David had travelled with a team, which he had increasingly come to believe was an inspired way to lead evangelistic festivals and missions. His team did not include the experts in administration, public relations,

follow-up, and research whom he might perhaps have needed if he had developed as a sort of British Billy Graham. David's team were not backstage staff but supporting cast. They provided music and drama and dance to illustrate the message and to lead the people in worship. They also provided counselling, and they were a resource for the various seminars which were part of the package for the festivals. They were as much a part of David's ministry as his own preaching, and so their spiritual quality was of the greatest importance.

The recruitment of the team was not altogether easy because he couldn't pick them out of his own congregation, though Diana Nairne transferred from the old York team and became especially valuable in helping to establish the right ethos in the new London team. David had also recruited a couple from Fuller Seminary; Mark Slomka, a 'completed Jew' who was released by the Californian Presbytery for two years to work with David before taking up a local pastorate, and his wife Carol, who was very talented in music and drama. John Collins suggested several names from his own congregation of whom Shaun Islip, a professional musician and entertainer who had not long been a Christian, Mark Jennings, a commercial artist who was a born clown, and Jane Campion, an actress who joined for only a few months, were enrolled. To these were added Sandy Campbell, fresh from drama school, who was the perfect foil for Mark Jennings by virtue of a 'beanpole' stature and a 'bootface' countenance.

David was also anxious to add to his repertoire the art of dance as a means of Christian communication, and rejoiced to find two very willing and professional performers in Margot Evans, a vivacious Australian brunette, and Alison Charles, a petite and attractive blonde. Everybody did a bit of everything but Shaun directed the

music, Carol the drama, Margot the dance, and Mark Slomka was overall leader, a role which had the greater significance during David's illness and especially after his death. For this team we found various units of accommodation, but the majority were housed in a furnished house in Battersea rented from a Christian couple who were just moving to South Africa.

David and Anne, Fiona and Guy, arrived in London in August 1982 and took up residence in their new home with a pleasant cat coloured and called after a kipper, and a rather formidable old mongrel dog who was guaranteed to guard their estate against friends and enemies alike. A new chapter was about to begin. If I have described the preliminaries in very human terms without any mention of God—who made it all possible and whose clear call had prompted it in the first place—it must not be thought that the move was undertaken without that constant prayer which was characteristic of David and without which he felt himself powerless. Every detail was prayed over carefully and none of us felt that we were acting without clear instructions as far as these were available. In view of the events which were to follow, some of their friends in York have wondered if it had ever been right to move at all but neither David nor Anne have ever doubted this except in moments of deep anxiety or when under great pressure. Their confidence in God to be eternally with them and altogether trustworthy triumphed over the blackest despair. They may sometimes have been cast down, but they were never forsaken.

Some have doubted the wisdom of taking that particular house, but to them it was a very precious God-given home of their own where their family life could be enjoyed to the full. True, it was a little too small for them and Hilary, especially when David's illness made it

necessary for visitors to come and see him there. The Archbishop of Canterbury had to squeeze through a very crowded office to get to the stairs, and some other welcome visitors must have wondered why so much work needed to be done in such a small space, but the privilege of a private home right in the heart of London was something the family prized very highly.

The move to London had one side-effect which was very natural but not at all pleasant. They found themselves plunged into deep grief at the loss of their church rather as parents mourn the loss of their children. It was not the loss of their own status as leaders and greatly beloved founders of St Michael's, but the loss of the intimate fellowship they enjoyed with so many there and the loss of the joy of witnessing the growth of the fruit of their own ministry there. They had done seventeen years' hard labour for and with the Lord in York with all the pain and hardship that involves, and they had seen a church of great strength and potential emerge from nothing as a result of those labours and sufferings. They had personally chiselled out the principles and the practices by which that church should stand and grow, and they had taught them and fought for them and almost died for them during those long years.

They had come to be willing to be relieved of the great burden of St Michael's, had chosen and trained their own successors and had successfully handed everything over. But suddenly they were without them, and the pain of that bereavement was very great. They suffered the very human experience of mourning for their loved ones and they found it hard to be comforted.

Unfortunately this coincided with their attempt to become members of Holy Trinity, Brompton. As the weeks went by that autumn David was fulfilling his programme of Festivals, and greatly enjoying his new found freedom from parochial duties on Sundays, which enabled him to visit his mother and sister in the country and Guy at school. In addition he undertook occasional Sunday preaching at other London churches. The leaders at HTB became mystified that the membership which had been so carefully arranged months in advance was being honoured more in the breach than the observance. But whatever else was true, HTB was not St Michael's York. In fact HTB is a very large congregation, lively and youthful, with a strong charismatic life and an outstandingly effective ministry of evangelism. They stand just where David stood. Their leader, John Collins, is David's spiritual father and lifelong supporter. David was never critical of them and always full of admiration for their tremendous vitality and effectiveness. Indeed, how could he be otherwise? Yet he and his family in their present state of bereavement could not easily identify with that great happy crowd of young people who wanted to celebrate while they wanted to weep.

The problem was increased for him because their very strength made him feel redundant. If he had anything special to offer it was only a refinement of what was already there, and his zeal made him restless in a church where life abounded and he had little responsibility.

If a mistake had been made perhaps it was in deciding to join a church long before it became necessary. David's strong emphasis upon the importance of belonging to a local church and submitting to its leadership led him to act in this matter without first entering the circumstances where he might be able to discern God's will accurately. David had been warned by one or two who had made similar mistakes, but his determination to belong and his love for John led him to do something which was too difficult for him.

All other issues disappeared from view with the news

David received from his doctor on 5th January 1983, only four months after beginning his work in London. The shock waves which began in that consulting room were to have a quite devastating effect on all of us who were involved in his ministry and its promotion. Immediately of course we had to arrange for the fulfilment or cancellation of the bookings for the next few months, and then for the care of David personally as he underwent and recuperated from the major intestinal operation to remove a malignant tumour from his colon. The first proved far easier than might have been expected for David MacInnes, diocesan missioner of Birmingham, and David Prior, vicar of St Aldate's Church, Oxford, agreed to deputise for the gruelling courses that David had pioneered with his team at Fuller Theological Seminary, California. They led a fortnight each, MacInnes completing the tour with a weekend in Fort Lauderdale among the US army personnel there. This really was immediate action, for the team were just about packed and ready when David was at his doctor's, and the notice given to Prior to clear his own diary and catch the plane was only two days.

It fell to my lot as Chairman of the trustees to face and inspire a really shocked and dejected team. Mark and Carol Slomka had gone home for Christmas, but the remaining six were flying out they knew not quite where, nor to do just what, nor under whose leadership, and they felt they were deserting David in his hour of need. They responded marvellously to the challenge. Praise God, they flew, were met by the Slomkas who were even more shocked than they, and under the two deputies were very successful in their ministry. Whether Fuller were entirely satisfied I don't know, but they were invited back in 1984 and are reassembling to go again in 1985 under David MacInnes' leadership.

The trustees decided immediately, even before the operation, that however good David's post-operative recovery might be he must take at least six months off, which when added to summer holidays would mean almost eight. Remarkably Douglas Greenfield, who administered all the festivals and tours, was staying in the south with Bob Roxburgh, minister of Millmead Centre, Guildford, when David's news broke, and together they discussed the possibility of Bob taking on many of the British bookings with the team for the next six months. David was thrilled to have such an offer, the Millmead deacons released Bob for it and the trustees gratefully accepted him. Eventually David MacInnes did one or two of these bookings and Bob the rest. It was an amazing God-given provision. These men are not easily available and their willingness to help us was the more remarkable.

During David's time in hospital Anne really showed her true mettle. Tireless in visiting him, confident on every decision to be made, cheerful and surprisingly relaxed, she took it all in her stride, and with no sign of panic even when the surgeon revealed that secondaries had been found in David's liver and this meant a life expectancy of about twelve months. Fiona quietly went on with her work and showed us all a smiling face. When I went to Guy's school to tell him that his father was very ill he received it with comparative calm. They were not unmoved by the threatening danger and they all loved David very deeply indeed, but his own acceptance of suffering and his dedication to his work over many years had made him someone whose fame and frequent absences set him a little apart. He was not personally remote in the very least, but they had had to learn to manage without him so much that news of some fresh disaster to him took a little time to sink in.

David's extraordinary appetite for work and unfailing dedication to those to whom he ministered perhaps inevitably resulted in an unusual family life. He was a personification of the so-called Protestant work ethic (he worked late into the night and was often at his desk again by six in the morning) but he was not generally available to his family as a father usually is. Anne's expressed opinion is that they only began to live properly as a family when they came to London, and if that is so it is sufficient explanation of why the Lord called them there for the last two years of David's life. They began to spend some time together and to go out together. David had been educated like his father before him at Wellington College in Berkshire, a distinguished public school where he achieved great distinction himself, and all his plans were for Guy to follow in his footsteps. Bitter indeed was the disappointment when the headmaster most apologetically advised David that this was not the right school for Guy. When the family moved to London another school was found, which has proved to be exactly right for Guy who has been very happy there. David learnt that a son would not necessarily benefit from following his father too exactly. Thus and in other ways the rigour of his personal rule of life gave way to a fuller and more relaxed enjoyment of God's goodness.

The first person after Anne whom David informed of his illness was John Wimber, pastor of Vineyard Christian Fellowship in California. He and David had developed across the world a remarkable affinity based on infrequent visits to each other. It was a 'David and Jonathan' relationship in which they enjoyed each other's complete confidence and shared each other's vision and principles of ministry. They were both fearless in faith and possessed greatness beyond their fellows as leaders in God's church. John Wimber's special emphasis is upon the importance of 'signs and wonders' in the Church as a God-appointed means of building a true Christian community, and the Vineyard has learnt to expect and to experience supernatural interventions into modern life similar to those described in the New Testament. There can be no argument that they frequently see miracles of healing taking place in their fellowship, some more remarkable than others, some of lasting value, some of temporary effect. Never have they seen or thought to see healed every person for whom they pray, nor every circumstance changed. They do not do the healing, God does, and they are only his agents in the process. God, it seems, does not always heal, being limited by the fallen nature of the world, but John Wimber believes that part of the Christian witness is to the signs and wonders which God does give for our edification and relief, and that Christian ministry should include this integral part of the work of the kingdom. Without it we are liable to lapse into a sub-Christian ministry at some point.

When David had had his operation John Wimber and two of his colleagues, John McClure and Blaine Cook, flew specially to London to pray with him. Their visit was a very great joy to him, and when they had prayed with him he was quite obviously enormously encouraged. They believed that they had experienced and had seen in him the sort of signs that were familiar to them on occasions when healing takes place within the body of a sufferer. They believed they had accomplished their mission in coming. Because they are equally experienced in seeing no healing take place, they never told him that they believed he was healed and he never thought they had. For the rest of his life David had no *certainty* that he had been healed, but he continued to pray and to ask for prayer for healing to take place.

I make this point because there has been some misunderstanding of this visit and its effects. Those who do not like so strong an emphasis upon healing may be tempted to believe that it is too nice a distinction to make between a healing and healing signs. The signs in this case were the peace and fulfilment experience by those who came to minister, and the physical warmth and energy which David felt coursing through his body. They were very similar to the signs experienced by ministers and patients when a miraculous healing does indeed take place, very common experiences for John Wimber and his friends, and not unknown even by myself. I take it that this is what was meant by Jesus when he spoke of virtue or power having gone out of him in Luke 8.46.

In David's case however at no stage was a clear claim of a healing made, and faith rested only upon the Lord's sovereign right to work his will one way or another. John was very content to have it so and believed his visit had been rewarding in that sense only; unless God tells him that healing has taken place or will take place, he never claims it and his integrity is bound up with this discipline. He experiences clear words of knowledge about various wonders and healings, and is privileged to see so many of them that it would be completely out of character for him to have told David he was healed without such knowledge. In point of fact we never heard from John or from anyone else that David was being healed or would be healed, though we and countless others across the world prayed that he would be, right up to the day of his death.

After this a more cheerful David made splendid progress and was soon home again. Anne took charge of him with her mother's help and he was able to take up a more normal though much quieter life. Gradually we began to discuss the future. His surgeon had told him that the inoperable condition of his liver would probably allow him another twelve months of life, but that he should refuse to accept that as a sentence and should go out to fight the cancer by embarking upon his ministry as though he had years ahead of him. He was to book up 1984 and beyond. This is the most therapeutic action to be taken to defeat cancer, and many have survived for far longer than expected because they have refused to give in to it. Some appear to have overcome it altogether. If David could set his sights on the future and devote himself to his ministry while the Church prayed on for his healing, surely there could be hope of some success at least.

But this presented his trustees with real problems. I wonder whether David's doctors realised how obsessional a worker he was, and how self-destructive was his normal schedule of activity. I counselled a radical change in programme and method, so that travelling could be cut to a minimum and the greatest strategic value could be gained from his talents, his experience and his remaining energies, at least for the next year or more. Douglas Greenfield pointed out that when a festival in a city was being planned enormous quantities of work were involved locally, and the pledging of considerable funds for publicity and other purposes was needed. Festivals were booked usually for three or four years ahead. Could we seriously consider such a timescale? There was also the question of the team, who still existed and needed employment and payment. David could not see himself bereft of the team who had by now become his church family, the residue of the great flock at York, but there was no sense in keeping them going, even if we could effectively do so, and in having to find substitutes to lead them. The tail would be wagging the dog. If we maintained them and made bookings for their ministry, it could only be with David as their leader, and if he was

194

away with them he could not learn to live at the gentler pace we believed he needed to adopt.

We did three things. First we circulated a newsletter telling our constituency that we could and would take bookings for David and his team only if those booking him accepted with us the 'risk of faith' that the booking might not be fulfilled. This was, I believe, very well received and took much of the tension out of all our dealings with those who looked for David's ministry to be continued as before. Secondly, David asked John Collins to release him from any membership at HTB though not from fellowship with them or from any preaching there which might be mutually arranged, so that he might look for a ministry in London for himself where he might perhaps be heard preaching regularly. Thirdly, David asked the Bishop of London if he could offer him a ministry of this sort, not looking for anything very flourishing, but a strategic centre where he and his team could begin in a small way without complication to build up God's work. The Bishop very kindly discussed various possibilities with him, though none were immediately available except one which for other reasons was not really suitable. Then the Bishop warmly recommended him to work with me at St Michael's, Chester Square.

I had realised that this was one obvious solution. Our St Michael's (in London, not York) is a fine building capable of seating about a thousand people, but designed so as to be 'cosy' for a few hundred. David and Anne worshipped there occasionally and he regarded us as 'having potential', by which he meant there was a great deal to be done there, which excited him. We were a small fellowship of Christians moving forward towards a fuller experience of Christian living and able to receive the sort of ministry David would offer. Some of our members knew the Watsons personally since their home was very near us, and no obvious difficulties were apparent. I began to sound out our leaders about the possibility of David coming to join us as the Bishop had suggested, but immediately discovered that it was one thing to have David live near by and preach for us from time to time, and quite another to make any formal arrangement concerning him without raising all sorts of questions. Looked at from a point more than a year later when David has been dead for six months, these difficulties seem petty and almost absurd, but at the time they assumed considerable proportions which frustrated me and depressed David. In the end we agreed to proceed slowly to a particular pattern, but this was not really what David needed, which was to find a pulpit for himself and a platform for his team where they could begin a new phase of ministry as soon as possible.

Meanwhile he had broken the trustees' embargo by giving an interview to Nick Page which was broadcast on BBC Radio 4 in April—'*A Case for Healing*'. It was a memorable and powerful account of his experiences as a cancer patient, of how he reconciled this with Christian faith, and of how he hoped for healing but could not be certain of it. Possibly he had never done anything so valuable before. David's great voice responding confidently and with superb balance to Nick's excellent questioning made this recording one of the best ever. It was repeated by popular request about a month later, and tapes of it have gone out round the world since. It still inspires many a failing sufferer and many a timorous believer.

As his strength returned in the early summer of 1983 he began to go again to meet people in various groups and to plan an autumn programme which, to Anne's despair, would plunge him back into speaking and travelling. He had some festivals booked, including one in Switzerland in September. He would again go to the Houses of Parliament where he had been asked to attend as a friend and adviser the regular meetings of the Parliamentary Wives' Group. He accepted two bookings for lunchtime meetings, one in the City for men, and one at the Hurlingham Club for women. What else was he to do? His doctors told him to work and the Church provided no other work for him to do. His beloved team was raring to go and he simply loved to minister. Actually many of his bookings did not include his team and he began to arrange others which would use them. In January 1984 he would go again to Fuller, in Lent he would try to fulfil engagements he had cancelled for 1983 and take on a course of teaching at St Paul's, Robert Adam Street. In July 1984 he would go for a course to Regents College, Vancouver, which had been put together around the ministry he and his team would offer.

In July 1983 he began a little light work and led one festival at Dartford. In August we went off together for a joint family holiday in a lovely house in Scotland. David and Anne with their family drove via York, where they spent the weekend, and David preached at St Michael's. David's back hurt him, the result, he thought, of twisting it a bit picking something up in his study at home. Anne had to do most of the driving but they very much enjoyed the holiday and David walked quite a bit in the glen. It was an idyllic setting. Most of the time the sun shone on us out of a bright blue sky, but one day the rains fell with tremendous effect, every gully and stream was white with turbulent water and the river flowed furiously over its banks. The next day all was calm again. We ate the trout Guy pulled ashore with great enthusiasm and tried out various Scottish delicacies including even haggis. We inspected Loch Ness and missed the ferry to the Isle of Skye by a very small but irretrievable margin.

David began work in September as though he had never left off, in spite of increasing pain in his back. Early in November one or two of us went to pray with him for it and he had immediate release from pain, which greatly delighted him and us. Next day his asthma started up and it proved to be an attack more severe than he had had before. His doctor put him on to a course of steroids which in the past had proved very quickly to be the answer to the asthma. This time it had little effect. Far from well he knew he should slow down, but he had to fulfil a booking in Ireland, where his ministry had always been very effective. Once more his ministry proved to be in his own words 'exceptionally fruitful', but thrush developed in his mouth and he had to surrender the final address to Cecil Kerr, who had arranged the visit. He came home rather dejected, the asthma still rampant, the thrush quite painful, and his feet very swollen from the effect of the steroids. But his faith was his first concern and he determined to go again to California to see John Wimber.

David was in fact approaching a crisis of faith comparable to that which he had experienced when undergoing his operation and facing an early death. This one was even more profound, for he was challenged on the quality of his relationship with God while still living, and not so much upon whether he was ready to die. The asthma continued throughout November and his inability to sleep gave him opportunity to pray and meditate. In the early hours of Advent Sunday, 27th November, he faced God with new freedom and found himself humbled as never before. Every part of his life and ministry including his personal relationships came under the Lord's gentle scrutiny. Nothing was allowed to come between him and his God. *'Seek my face'* was the challenge of the Lord.

This was the classic Christian experience of which we are told infrequently but which doubtless comes to a great many. From time to time it is movingly recorded for us in each generation. The Christian who will patiently seek the Lord, counting 'all things but loss for the excellency of the knowledge of Christ Jesus' shall surely find him. This is no weak introspection, but the genuine mystical experience of the living God entering human life. It is not limited to any branch, tradition or emphasis within Christendom; it is not the product of any programme, nor is it characteristic of any one section nor the inheritance of any particular group. It is the fulness of Christ, freely available to every Christian. Painful as David found the experience and as it seemed, perhaps, to those who heard him tell of it, it liberated him finally from any man-made or self-imposed sense of responsibility. From henceforth he would serve Christ only.

Margaret and I had told David that if Anne couldn't manage it, we would go with him to California any time he wanted. We flew out on the afternoon of 1st December arriving at Los Angeles Airport in the early evening of the same day (by time loss!) to be met by John Wimber himself. There followed a remarkable week. David stayed with the Wimbers and no doubt much passed between them which confirmed and illuminated his new found liberty and joy. John Wimber is a gentle loving bear of a man! I have no doubt at all that for David that week with John, and with Carol his wife, was a precious time in which their own friendship was enriched by their open discussion of what the future held for David. Most of the days were given up to prayer by different groups from the Vineyard for David's healing. I remember John crying out to the Lord. I remember John McClure kneeling bolt upright for two hours beside David's recumbent form. I remember the sweet quietness of the prayers of Penny Fulton, Carol's sister. Every day they prayed and we with them. There were always people carefully seeing that we were feeling welcome and being appropriately entertained, and one day they insisted that Margaret and I went to Disneyland. The basic pre-occupation, however, was with David's healing which transcended all other commitments.

It was at the Vineyard that David came to see himself afresh as God's son. His own father had died when he had been very young and he had never known a loving father on earth as most people do. He tried to accept fatherly love and leadership from different people at different times, but they tended rather naturally to fail him in some respects for he set such high standards. To be able to relax into the everlasting arms of his heavenly Father was to have one great problem solved. It was also at the Vineyard that he clearly faced the probability of death before very long, though he never stopped praying expectantly for healing. He came to recognise how much his family meant to him and rather shyly commissioned us to see they would be all right. But it was at the Vineyard, while the most intense and explicit praying for his healing was going on, that his physical condition deteriorated most sharply. His abdomen started to expand almost visibly and his asthma continued to keep him awake at night. His feet and ankles were still swollen and we wondered if the abdomen too might have been swollen from water retention caused by the steroids, but his body began to show the wasting effect of cancer upon the human frame. It was as though the Lord in his wisdom was showing to his dear faithful people that his answer to their prayers would in this case be 'No'.

When we returned it was with a markedly weaker but more peaceful David, who met his trustees as cheerfully as ever, and very obediently accepted their decisions to cancel his future engagements and disband the team as soon as they had fulfilled theirs. It was done as gently as possible, and it was no real surprise to him, but it was of course the end of an era and a bitter disappointment. He went home to his family to finish *Fear No Evil* and to wait prayerfully for the Lord's will to be revealed. With extraordinary strength he fulfilled some commitments for *In Company* on TV South but on Christmas Day he was too weak to come to dinner with us. He told a friend 'I feel I have one foot in heaven and one on earth and I'm happy to land on either foot.'

On 7th March 1984, which would have been David's 51st birthday, we sent out a Belfrey Trust Newsletter from which I quote the following extract:

David Watson died very early on Saturday 18th February 1984. At the beginning of January he had sent out a newsletter describing his condition and inviting his friends to pray with him for healing and victory. He preached twice more in our church, St Michael's Chester Square, on 8th and 15th January. Each sermon lasted a good half-hour and was delivered in that familiar strong voice with the usual clarity of thought and expression, the delightful touches of humour and the compelling personal references. On the 15th he went home very exhausted. His strength seemed to fail from that hour. But as you would expect the sermons were marvellous exhortations to faith and discipleship, to courage and endurance against every foe. 'The best is yet to be' he repeated, and 'you are my God; in you I trust'. The frail figure perched on a high stool held every eye and ear and heart.

He continued to see close friends and family during the last month and to pray, and to ask others to pray for his healing. To the very end we did. The Bishop of London came and the Archbishop of Canterbury ('I just want to thank him for all

201

he has done for faith among God's people'). Bishop Morris Maddocks brought him Holy Communion, and David MacInnes came when he got back from Fuller. David said to him with a grin: 'I am completely at peace. There is nothing I want more than to go to heaven. I know how good it is.' Later the team returned and went to see him two by two, though he could only manage a few minutes with them. All the time Anne nursed him with the expert help of her mother, and Fiona's invaluable support. The wasting and weakening disease took its steady course, pain-killing drugs prevented any great distress, though for a short while they seemed to confuse his mind a little. For the final ten days he was lucid and alert, fully aware of what was happening and able to discuss it with his children.

On Friday 17th I went to see him and prayed for his healing, sitting holding his hand afterwards for about five minutes. The doctor came and spoke gravely. Guy came home for half-term and had a bright conversation with David about hockey and the team he was in, to their mutual delight. In the evening he said to Anne 'I'm very tired; let's go home'. She was in no doubt as to what he meant. She went to bed leaving her mother to stay with him, but praying that God would wake her up to be with him before he died. She woke at midnight. He died fifteen minutes later.

Anne asked the Lord for a verse to strengthen her and read Isaiah 26.19:

Those who belong to God shall live again.
Their bodies shall rise again.
Those who dwell in the dust shall awake and sing for joy!
For God's light of life will fall like dew upon them.

Why was he not healed? On the BBC Sunday programme on 19th February David MacInnes was asked that question and replied 'If I knew the answer to that, I should be God'. Throughout the last year of David's life he had repeatedly said he believed God could heal him and wanted to heal him. He said 'I believe I am being healed, but I could be wrong'. To the last day we prayed for healing and asked everyone else to do so too. Were we wrong? I have heard it said that David has died because we did not have enough faith. Exactly how much should we have had? If I have sometimes faltered as I have been so close to the actual physical evidence of David's illness, I believe God has been well pleased with the prayers of that great worldwide company of believing praying people who have persisted sacrificially over many months. But it is not our prayers or our faith which heal. God heals. After all, prayer is not instructing God in his duties or ordering from him what we want. It is co-operating with him in fulfilling his purposes to which we must humbly submit. He reigns—we serve. So I do not know why David was not healed, but I do know we were called to pray for it, and though God did not respond as we hoped we cannot have been wrong in praying. Nor was our weak faith the determining factor, but rather God's sovereign grace.

Was it then a victory for the devil? I can well believe the devil's disciples were glad to see the back of David Watson, but actually the devil has no power and can win no victories unless they be 'given from on high'. It is nonsense, sheer nonsense to believe in any victory for Satan over Christ and his Church. In 2 Tim. 4.6–8 Paul wrote of his early expectation of a violent death. But he states confidently that 'the Lord will rescue me from all evil and save me for his heavenly kingdom' (verse 18). His death was not a victory for evil, but gave glory to God. Through history God has not protected his Church from suffering and many of his saints have had to endure a painful death. So did Christ. That's where our victory lies. The only victory for Satan would be if we behaved as though David's death were the end of the story instead of the beginning of a new chapter of victories. The Lord reigns and his kingdom will prosper.

Why then has David been taken? Why should he not have been? We Christians do not see death as any sort of disaster or penalty, but as a natural step into the life eternal. As I said at the little service we had for David's funeral, 'hockey one minute—heaven the next!' It must be hard for unbelievers to be so relaxed about it, but not for those who are God's heirs.

The ceaseless labours and sufferings of David's ministry deserved an early end. But why have we lost our leader? David lived with this tension between going home and staying on. He naturally would have loved to stay with those he loved and he believed there was so much more work for him to do for Christ. It was like the tension of praying with faith for healing and seeing the physical signs of approaching death. All our lives we Christians live with similar tensions between the material and the spiritual (2 Cor. 5.1–10). But we walk by faith not by sight, and now by faith we joyfully accept the divine decision, even if we do so with tears. Personally I have lost a greatly beloved brother, but that is nothing compared to the loss which the Church has suffered. I do not understand at all why, in the prime of life, he is taken. But God has so chosen and thanks be to God.

Murray Watts, a friend and colleague at York, heard it said in a local pub that 'if God couldn't heal David Watson, who could he heal?' I do not want to comment on the basic error in the statement that God, being a respecter of persons, might award healing as a prize for loyal service. God has chosen to be limited in his capacity to bless us by our capacity, or the lack of it, to receive that blessing. I believe with all my heart that our prayers and fastings came up before God as a sweet sacrifice of love and were acceptable. All over the world people prayed for weeks and months on end for this healing to be given. But, I ask myself, what would have happened if David had been healed? Already David was fighting off the personality cult which is the enemy of the Christian ministry. Endless invasions of his private life had to be defeated, and many Christians regarded him as some sort of infallible guru to be heard and obeyed whenever possible. Once when the family were in church together a young lady from the pew behind asked Anne, 'Do you actually know David Watson?' This sort of tendency may be only a nuisance to star performers in other fields, but for the preacher it is so counter-productive as to be positively destructive. He who preaches Christ cannot accept worship of himself and must become so careful about publicity that he avoids any danger of self-exaltation.

If David had been healed, could the Church have received him back as from death itself without blasphemy? Could we have found a new role for him without imposing quite intolerable burdens upon him? Could we have accurately interpreted the event without building a totally unbalanced doctrine of the ministry of healing? What would have been the reputation of the minister, if any, through whom the healing had been given? What if John Wimber, if it had been he? He would probably have survived admirably, but what if it had been me? Or the young theological student who sometimes came with me to pray for David? Would our lives and ministries have been possible in the subsequent blaze of publicity? Was there more for David to do?

Obviously there is much more to be done in the Church today and David was especially gifted to meet our greatest needs. He cannot but be missed most grievously. But before we start feeling too sorry for ourselves perhaps we should make the most of the enormous legacy he has left us on paper and on tape. As Anne has said, 'God has his own plan for the Church and we must leave David to enjoy the happiness which is now his.' We each have our own call to our own ministry, and we might do well to concentrate our thoughts for a while upon those very areas of growth in David which marked his last year.

During his illness David changed in certain respects that are highly significant. As a family man he developed a new sensitivity and realism in his relationships with people. He became a very much more whole person, showing that healing, which he did not receive, and wholeness, which he did, are not the same thing. I believe that the Church too needs to experience this development of personality under the hand of God, so that within the local church really loving relationships between believers, free from inhibitions or prejudices of every sort, can be established for all to see. Is not this the purpose for which the Church was founded? 'By this shall all men know that you are my disciples, if you have love one for another.' We Christians should be obsessed with loving one another.

As a minister David developed from being the giver to being the receiver. Formerly the strong and enormously compelling speaker and writer, equipped with every gift of communication, zealous to discharge his commission to everyone who could be brought to hear. Latterly the weak and wasted invalid dependent upon others for everything—upon God, of course, for salvation and for healing if he would; upon those near to him for daily encouragement and succour; upon the worldwide Church for prayer. The Church needs to recapture its role as the receiver rather than the giver. We are determined to force our own arrogant opinions and remedies upon a dying world, forgetful of the fact that Christianity is a *given* religion. We Christians must *receive* God's love and truth for transmission to his world.

In his ministry David had sought by every means in his power to promote the unity of the Church by proclaiming the sovereignty of Christ over all. He had not taken part so much in ecumenical discussions, but he had insisted upon expressing the unity of the Body of Christ wherever he went. In his last year of life he attracted the united prayers of Christians the world over across every man-made boundary. Every Christian could claim David as a brother and could share a concern for him with every other. After his death two great cathedrals in England held services of thanksgiving for his life, attended by capacity congregations from every walk of life and led by the two Archbishops. Many other services were held in many places. This unity of the Church must go on being expressed by our promotion of the causes of the kingdom. We cannot hope to demolish the terrible barriers of the world or bridge the yawning fissures within it if, as the Church of the one Lord Jesus Christ, we ourselves are torn apart. Our leaders must discern the great causes behind which we can unite and call us to pray for them and to work for them. The kingdom of God is not divided, and yet *we* are obsessed with our divisions.

If the body of David Watson became a battleground for these issues, his death remains a glorious victory. The fight was grievous while it lasted, but from it David has been released into the presence of his loving Father who always retained full control of every detail. Will the Church fight on with the same unflinching courage?

The best is yet to be.

APPENDIX

The Most Reverend Lord Blanch was Archbishop of York during the latter part of David Watson's ministry in the city. He gave this address at the Thanksgiving Service held in York Minster on 17th March 1984.

'He was a burning and shining lamp and you were willing for a season to rejoice in his light.' This was our Lord's tribute to John the Baptist, and I suppose he might be saying the same of David today. At first sight there is more by way of contrast than similarity between John the Baptist and David. Even in the most extreme straits of family life I doubt whether David was ever reduced to locusts and wild honey!

John the Baptist was a man of the desert; that was his true habitat and a suitable place for the kind of fierce spirituality which he enjoyed. David was perhaps more like Elisha, going in and out among the people, carrying his own 'desert' with him as we all do, but no lean ascetic. John the Baptist was accustomed to what seems to us an outlandish dress—camel's hair and a leathern girdle. It was one of the persistent jokes between David and myself that I always said to him, 'David, you're looking every inch an Archdeacon today.' I never saw him looking otherwise, always impeccably even if modestly attired.

The similarities are, however, more striking than the contrasts. John the Baptist was sent to prepare the way of the Lord, which he did faithfully. David all his life was preparing the way for the Lord, making a passage for him into the lives of others—with his sermons; with his seventeen books; in private counselling; in public ministry at home and abroad, always making it easier for people to believe in God. And that is what an evangelist is—not necessarily a person with a striking style; not always a person with great charismatic gifts, but one who makes it easier for others to believe in God.

But like John the Baptist, David of course had to pay the price: he had to grow less. There is a sense in which every minister of the gospel is diminished by his ministry. If he has any self-knowledge at all, his ministry makes him less confident in himself, less assured, less doctrinaire and therefore sometimes less secure. He becomes more aware of the dark places in his own life and in the lives of others. Anyone who has been long in the ministry will know the time when he has to say, 'I stumble where once I firmly trod.' Every John Baptist has his own 'Machaerus', that grim forbidding fortress in the Judaean desert, the place of fear and doubt and spiritual imprisonment. But through it all, David never proposed for himself anything other than the will of God. Of course he was occasionally, as everyone else, mistaken about what the will of God was, but he never sought to evade it and he never ceased to seek it. The cost of discipleship of that kind is very high; there is no cheap grace.

He was a burning and a shining light. I suppose what most impressed people when they went to St Michael's was the extent to which David himself remained a student and expositor of the Scriptures. This steady process of study and exposition constitutes the basis of all ministry, as I believe it did of David's. His study was not of the academic kind, removed from life. It was a struggle to understand the inexplicable, the struggle to express the inexpressible: the struggle to penetrate the ineffable mystery of Christ.

It used to be said that if you went to hear Robertson of Brighton preaching you came away saying to yourself, 'What a wonderful man!' If you went to hear Spurgeon speak, and if you went to hear David speak, you came away saying, 'What a wonderful Saviour!' This is the difference between the great preacher and the great preacher who suffers in the process of the preparation for and the delivery of his sermons.

David was also a burning and shining light for the Church, and for the Church of England in particular, which he loved. He was never content just to exercise his own ministry, to go it alone. He was persistently concerned to establish a well-equipped ministry amongst the congregation; to create a loving and witnessing congregation and a warm, friendly worshipping community. St Michael's never was, and I pray never will be, a conventicle for like-minded people. It is part of the great Church to which it belongs, and to which it gives particular expression. My first meeting with the elders of the church, who were drawn from a variety of Christian institutions, was a very happy affair. They said to me at the end of the discussion, 'Of course Archbishop we accept your authority without question, because you are David's Archbishop.' This I think was the attraction of St Michael's for young and old, wise and foolish, for the successful and the failures. They were not drawn just by David, but by the palpable presence of God there in the midst.

David was a burning and a shining light also for the world. He stood for a city set on a hill which cannot be hid. He stood for a lamp on a lampstand, for the illumination of the world, not just for the edification of the Church or for the enjoyment of a private vision. It was a church concerned for the desperate social needs of our society—the lonely, the disturbed, the addicts, the homeless. Thank God that St Michael's never was the place where the needy man was told 'Go in peace; be warmed and filled', without ever being given any assistance for either.

We rejoiced with him for a season and I suppose many of us here could have wished it was longer. He was a shining and a burning light, but shining and burning is a costly business and it took its toll. The kind of life which David lived called for a robust physical constitution that he never enjoyed. It called for arduous intellectual effort, and one ought never to minimise that element in the life of any true evangelist. It called for painful spiritual self-knowledge. The kind of life he lived would expose any man to spiritual bankruptcy if he should ever lose hold of the unsearchable riches of Christ. There was also a cost to be paid in terms of the demands of the community as a whole and of the team in particular. Inevitable tensions, fragile relationships, shallow enthusiasms and moral hazards called for patience and sympathy, and like every leader, David sometimes had to take extremely disagreeable decisions. And then there were the demands of overseas travel. He was frequently away from his home, separated too often from his family, and fatigued as we all are by jet travel. David sometimes became the victim of enthusiastic but unthinking hospitality, and suffered from the inner exhaustion which sometimes follows dazzling outward success. There are times when the dazzling outward success only deepens the sense of inner depression and despair.

We ask therefore, 'What were the secrets of David's ministry?' Of him I suppose as much as of anybody it could be said that 'to live was Christ.' That is one of the most extraordinary utterances of St Paul. 'For him to live was Christ', four Greek words which expressed everything that St Paul understood about himself and about his ministry—'Not I but Christ.' He was aware that he had that treasure in a fragile earthen vessel, always carrying about in his body the death of Jesus, that the life of Jesus also might be manifested. So also David, aware of his own frail physical constitution and knowing the demands that were made upon him, was yet convinced that it was right to go on, having in his heart the assurance of eternal life.

In Ecclesiastes 12 we find some haunting images of death:

> The keepers of the house tremble, and the strong men are bent; when the grinders cease because they are few, and those who look through the windows are dimmed; when the doors on the street are shut; when the sound of the grinders is low, and one rises up at the voice of a bird; when all the daughters of song are brought low; when men are afraid also of what is high and terrors are in the way; when the almond tree blossoms, the grasshopper drags itself along, and desire fails, then man goes to his eternal home.

Perhaps David's greatest resource of all was that he knew that he would go to his eternal home and find his Father waiting for him.

BOOKS BY DAVID WATSON

Published by Hodder and Stoughton:
One in the Spirit
I Believe in Evangelism
I Believe in the Church
Is Anyone There?
Discipleship
Through the Year with David Watson
You Are My God
Fear No Evil

Published by Falcon/Kingsway:
My God is Real
In Search of God
Start a New Life (Booklet)
Be Filled with the Spirit (Booklet)

Published by IVP:
Live a New Life

Published by Send the Light:
Hidden Warfare

Published by Lion:
Jesus then and now

MESSAGE AND VIDEO CASSETTES

For the complete catalogue of talks by David
Watson which have been made available on
cassette, please write to Anchor Recordings,
72 The Street, Kennington, Ashford, Kent
TN24 9HS, or telephone Ashford 20958.

THE ADVENTURE
OF LIVING

Paul Tournier

Dr Paul Tournier, now retired, was a general practitioner in Geneva for nearly fifty years. Here he explains that God guides us when we are on the way, not when we are standing still, just as one cannot steer a car unless it is moving.

'Despite our uncertainties and our vagueness, even through our failings and mistakes... He leads us step by step, from event to event.'

'The Bible gives adventure its true meaning, for from end to end it reveals what is at stake in all our work, all our activity, all our choices, and all our self-commitment.'

ESCAPE FROM LONELINESS

Paul Tournier

'It is our own secrets that separate us the most from others; remorse for our wrongdoings, fears that haunt us.'

A DOCTOR'S CASEBOOK
IN THE LIGHT
OF THE BIBLE

Paul Tournier

'Our profession is a priestly ministry. I should like to see the church consecrating doctors just as it ordains ministers. This would be in conformity with the gospel. It is the conviction which makes us give ourselves with our hearts and minds and souls to our vocation.'

'A work of the deepest spiritual insight.'

Church Times

WHAT IS A FAMILY?

Edith Schaeffer

In an age when the family is being threatened as never before, Edith Schaeffer presents a powerful reaffirmation of the joys of family life. She writes as wife, mother and grandmother at L'Abri, the Christian community in Switzerland.

EVANGELISM IN THE EARLY CHURCH

Michael Green

Canon Michael Green is both an evangelist and a New Testament scholar. This has enabled him to produce one of the finest books on this subject ever written.

'Expert... a most lucid examination.'

Daily Telegraph